THE HOME VIDEO BOOK

THE HOME VIDEO BOOK

BY BRUCE APAR
AND HENRY B. COHEN

AMPHOTO BOOKS
American Photographic Book Publishing
An Imprint of Watson-Guptill Publications
New York

Copyright © 1982 by Bruce Apar and Henry B. Cohen

First published in New York, New York, by American Photographic Book Publishing: an imprint of Watson-Guptill Publications, a division of Billboard Publications, Inc., 1515 Broadway, New York, NY 10036.

Library of Congress Cataloging in Publication Data

Apar, Bruce.
    The home video book.

    Includes index.
    1. Home video systems. I. Cohen, Henry B. II. Title.
TK9961.A6   621.388'33   82-1650
ISBN 0-8174-3990-0   AACR2
ISBN 0-8174-3991-9 (pbk.)

Manufactured in the United States of America

First Printing, 1982

1 2 3 4 5 6 7 8 9 / 87 86 85 84 83 82

For Mom, Dad, Robert, and Stephen.

*And for a very special source of
inspiration & love,
Dale Kalikow*

Special thanks for the invaluable help provided to the authors by Annette Lazzarino; to John Bailey, for putting in a good word; to Mike O'Connor and Micaela Rosenzweig, for patience, understanding, and professionalism; and to William A. Burton and Philip A. Ambrosino, a deep debt of gratitude from Henry Cohen for the kind of indispensable support and friendship that helped make this effort possible.

CONTENTS

INTRODUCTION

The Home Video Book is unlike any other home video guide ever written. In this book, the authors explain home video in the simplest of terms so that the home video user has a complete, wealth of useful video knowledge at his or her fingertips. Explanations have been kept practical, hands-on guidance has been emphasized.

A complete section on the history of home video and its future is included to help place the entire field of interest in perspective.

The book is also unique in that it addresses home video components, the television set, the videocassette recorder and the video camera, in general and not by specific brands. This will help readers understand how these various pieces of equipment work without having to continually refer to owner's manuals when they use equipment. We have also kept references to the various formats to a minimum because, as for brands, if you understand the basics you also understand the specifics.

Beyond an explanation of how to use each piece of equipment, *The Home Video Book* also describes in detail uses of accessories, shopping tips on buying equipment, installation and setups, tips on working with video cameras, production techniques, experimenting with special effects, and so on.

The Home Video Book takes you through post-production techniques, equipment maintenance, suggested applications and contains a glossary of the most often used video terms. *The Home Video Book* was written to be complete, yet not intimidating in any way. Throughout you will find that the authors assumed you knew little or nothing about home video and have explained it in easy-to-understand terms. After all, if you are savvy enough to purchase home video equipment, then with a little help you can surely operate it to its ultimate capacity. With this in mind, feel free to read this book in any order you desire.

THE EQUIPMENT

If you are a neophyte approaching video with a background in still photography or amateur moviemaking, or both, certain of the camera recording techniques and feature descriptions in this book will be familiar. Novice home video hobbyists with little or no substantial experience in any form of photography will want to make repeated references to those pages discussing video cameras and their use, as they first explore and then master the existing art of video movie making.

First, forget about film. The videotape used to record and play back images and sounds that you can easily view on a conventional television screen does not look, feel, or act like film. You will rarely, as a beginner, actually have physical contact with videotape. In home use (and in most professional applications) it is threaded around two hubs in a sealed, self-contained housing called a "videocassette." These cassettes range in dimension from the size of an audiocassette to that of an elongated paperback book. Upon close inspection, you will notice that the tape contained inside is a narrow brown strip with a shiny coating on one side and a dull, flat surface on the other side that is magnetically coated to record images and sound. In simpler terms, it looks, and is very much like, the tape used to make audiocassette recordings. There are no visible frames on videotape; it looks exactly the same whether it is blank or filled with images and sound. Also there are no sprocket holes like those found on movie film.

All this is to identify immediately the major differences between movie film and videotape. Film records and reproduces images chemically, while videotape records them electromagnetically. Understanding this explains why, with most current video equipment, the videotape is not inserted into the camera, as film is.

(Cameras designed to accept miniature videocassettes are now

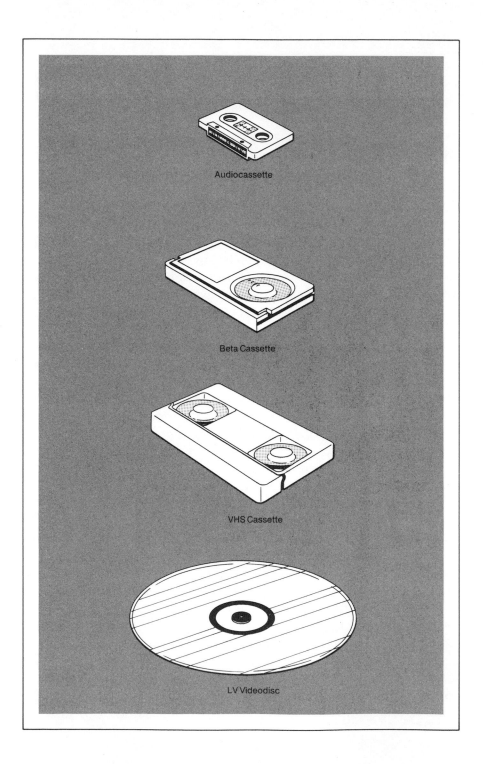

Audiocassette

Beta Cassette

VHS Cassette

LV Videodisc

being developed by major manufacturers of still photography, motion picture, and electronics equipment. In fact, a few professional camera/videocassette recorder combinations are currently on the market. Their enormous cost, however, places them out of range of all nonbroadcast users. In any case, the information contained in this book will remain applicable even through the next generation of single-piece video camera/recorders. You can read more about future products in chapter 7.)

Inside the video (or TV) camera is a light-sensitive electronic tube (known as Vidicon, Plumbicon, Saticon, or Newvicon) that sees the image you focus on and sends a series of electronic impulses through a cable that connects to a separate video recorder. Inside the recorder is the videocassette. When both camera and deck are working together, the videotape inside the cassette is moving, being unwound from the "feed" reel on the left and being wound onto the "take-up" reel on the right. With the tape moving in this manner, it is recording the images seen by the camera lens and the sounds heard by the microphone.

The most widespread misconception held by newcomers is that the tape itself goes inside the videocamera, or that you can use the camera by itself. The first rule to remember, then, is that the videotape cassette must be in the recorder, which, in turn, must be connected to the camera by a cable. Without this basic setup (camera, recorder, and tape), you cannot create recorded video images.

WHAT THE VCR CAN DO

The videocassette deck is used to record and play back moving color images, automatically synchronized with sound. It can record both prerecorded programs and live action (with a camera). Without a camera it can record from a television set or another videocassette deck or videodisc player that is playing back a program. It can also be used simply to play back a cassette you have purchased or rented in a store. (Like a record album, these cassettes are recorded commercially by professionals and are called "prerecorded" programs or tapes.)

When used to play back any of these programs, the videocassette recorder (VCR) must be connected to a television set, which allows you to watch whatever has been recorded on the cassette. Picture and sound will appear on the TV screen and loud-

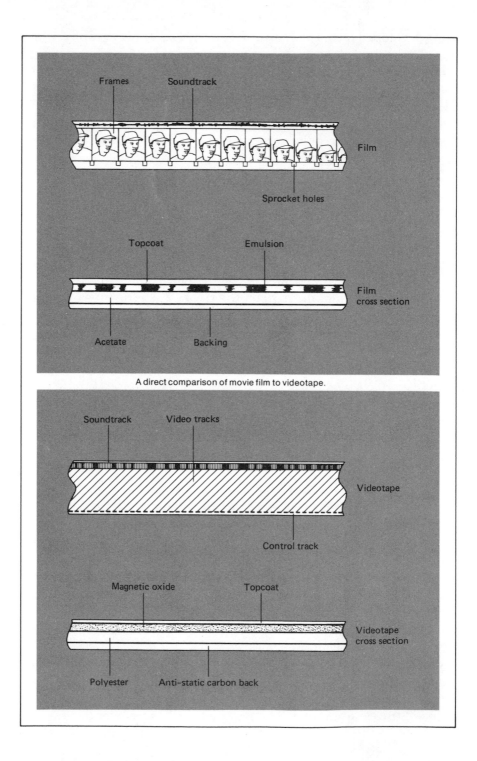

A direct comparison of movie film to videotape.

speaker just as they do when you tune in a channel to watch a program on regular broadcast television.

When referring to any kind of self-originated program (such as when playing back from a cassette), it is more precise to use the term "video" program rather than "television" program. The word *television,* in fact, is of Greek origin, and means "to see" [vision] something being sent from a "distance" [tele-]. This is how we will use our terminology throughout this book. You will naturally come to use it as you become more involved with video.

By reading this book you'll learn how to work actively with your equipment and creatively produce your own video programs— whether they are as simple as recording, compiling, and editing "off-air" television shows you may want to keep for nostalgic or historic reasons, or as involved as conceiving, planning, scripting, setting up, and recording, with a videocamera, your own home productions.

THE TV SET WITHOUT A SCREEN

The easiest way to record with a VCR, and to learn its features and overall operation, is to use it to videotape TV programs you want to save, or shows you want to watch but can't because you won't be home at the time of their scheduled broadcast.

To do this, think of your VCR as a television receiver without a viewing screen. It (or a separate, component tuner) has an antenna connection on its rear panel, so you can hook up your master or cable TV antenna directly to the VCR. The tuner section, self-contained or separate, has the same channel selection you have on your TV set. That's all you need to record broadcast ("off-air") or cable television programs. Because it has all the same internal electronics and channel selection features as a TV set, it is capable of receiving the same signals as your TV. The VCR by itself, then, is all you need to record broadcast ("off-air") or cable TV shows.

The television set becomes a necessary component of home video in a number of ways:

You want to watch (monitor) a program while you are taping the same program.

You want the VCR to record one program while you watch another being broadcast at the same time.

You want to watch the playback of any videocassette.

All of these viewing experiences, and any other combinations you discover as we go along, require a TV screen in order to watch the images your VCR is playing back from a videocassette. The TV set is *not* necessary, however, to *record* television programs on your VCR.

A VCR can be connected for playback through any kind of TV set, no matter how large the screen.

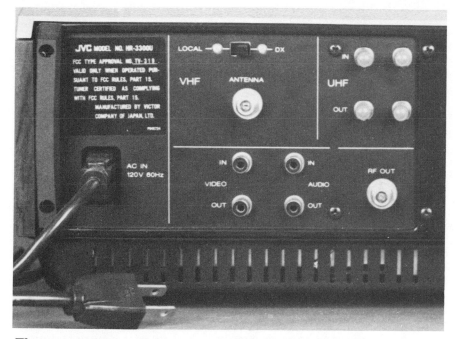

The rear panel of a VCR is where you'll find the terminals and jacks needed for setting up your connections—be it to the TV set, from an antenna, or to and from another VCR. The VHF antenna input accepts the master TV or cable TV antenna that would be hooked up to it for direct recording of programs. The RF OUTput jack is used to connect coaxial cable to your TV in order to play back through the TV. The audio and video INput/OUTput jacks can be used for a variety of applications. The output or camera control unit that is used when recording home movies connects to these plugs. If you were recording from or onto another VCR, or if you had a TV with direct audio/video inputs, these plugs would be used as well.

THE AUTOMATIC TIMER

How can the VCR record a television program if you're not at home to turn it on when the scheduled time arrives? In addition to its own tuner, the recorder has its own digital clock that functions as an automatic timer to turn on the recording mechanism, unattended. You may be sleeping, otherwise involved, or simply not at home—it matters not to your VCR.

If you spot a program in the TV listings that you want to view, but won't be home in time to watch it, simply:

Set the tuner of your VCR to the proper channel

Set the timer to go on (and off) at the prescribed times

Ensure that a videocassette is loaded into your VCR

. . . and you're all set.

THE VCR'S PROGRAMMABILITY

Now that you know the tuner and timer can perform "unattended recording" of a TV program, perhaps you're wondering about what happens if you plan to be away for a full week or more but don't want to miss a single episode of that engrossing soap opera that keeps you on the edge of your seat.

Enter the "multi-day" programmable tuner/timer. Depending upon the model, a VCR may be "programmed" to record the same channel at the same time every day for a number of consecutive days. When used in this manner, your VCR is being programmed "serially."

An even more flexible feature of programmability is that you can set some VCR models to record different channels at different times on nonconsecutive days. Or, it can be "preset" to record a number of different channels within the same day. There are many variations of the number of channels and days a VCR's programmability will allow for, depending on the brand and model of the VCR. About the only exception is that two separate channels cannot be recorded simultaneously by one VCR.

PORTABLE VCRS

A videocassette recorder with a tuner and timer built-in is called a "console" or "tabletop" AC model. A "portable" deck does not usually have the tuner and timer, but has a battery compartment, is made to run on 12 volts of DC power, and frequently sports a handle or shoulder strap. This type of VCR is, of course, lighter, smaller, and designed for use with a camera while on location—on a picnic, at the beach, or at a sporting event.

With portable decks the tuner and timer are usually packaged in a separate matching module that doubles as a battery recharger for the portable VCR, and as an AC adapter when you return home to watch your handiwork on the TV screen. When a portable VCR is reconnected to the tuner/timer, you can usually recharge the battery overnight—sometimes quicker.

Portable VCRs are more versatile in terms of power sources

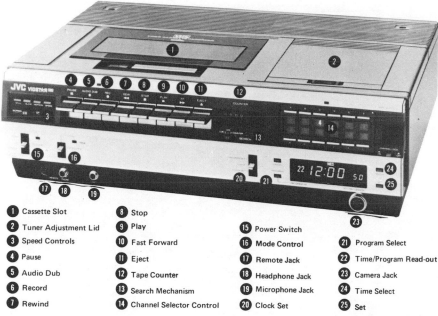

1 Cassette Slot	**8** Stop		
2 Tuner Adjustment Lid	**9** Play	**15** Power Switch	**23**
3 Speed Controls	**10** Fast Forward	**16** Mode Control	**21** Program Select
4 Pause	**11** Eject	**17** Remote Jack	**22** Time/Program Read-out
5 Audio Dub	**12** Tape Counter	**18** Headphone Jack	**23** Camera Jack
6 Record	**13** Search Mechanism	**19** Microphone Jack	**24** Time Select
7 Rewind	**14** Channel Selector Control	**20** Clock Set	**25** Set

Before using your VCR, it's best to familiarize yourself with all of its features, whether visible on the front panel, or hidden behind closed doors. Studying this illustration is a quick yet effective way to learn the basic functions of a typical VCR even before you enter the store. Other models, of course, may have more or fewer features, or the same features differently identified. In this picture the transport controls are mechanical, not electronic, while the channel selector (No. 14) is electronic.

than their stay-at-home counterparts. They can operate from AC power, their built-in rechargeable batteries, a separate power belt, or an automobile or a boat battery. For automobile or boat batteries use of a special connecting cord is necessary. These are available from the company that makes the VCR or from many electronics, video, and radio supply stores.

A video camera plugs directly into a portable VCR and both run for up to one hour on a single charge of the VCR's built-in battery. It's always a good idea to have a fully charged spare battery pack on hand if an hour of recording isn't long enough.

Since having a video camera means you'll most likely have—or want to use it with—a portable VCR, some people forget that a video camera can also be used with a homebound, tabletop VCR. Some tabletop models are similar to portables in that you can plug the camera directly into the recorder's camera connector. Other

Along with the electronic tuning selector, found on many new VCRs, comes a hidden compartment with fine tuning knobs that allow you to adjust each channel for optimum picture quality and reception. The tracking knob or skew control adjusts for slight tracking errors that may occur when playing a cassette made commercially or made on another recorder.

tabletop VCRs may not have a direct camera connection but rather have *AUDIO* and *VIDEO IN*put jacks. With this type of tabletop VCR, a video camera must be used with an AC adapter for the camera. The camera is plugged into the adapter, which is then connected to the VCR's audio/video input jacks. Because a console VCR is not designed to be moved easily, this situation is highly limiting to the aspiring video photographer—but it can be done. A serious home cameraman won't put up with it very long. If you are going into video this far, go portable.

Although they both perform most of the same functions, a portable VCR (bottom) is more versatile than its counterpart (top), the tabletop or console type of VCR. The tabletop version cannot operate via batteries, and is too heavy to be easily transported. Very few tabletop models offer direct camera inputs. Most require a camera control unit (CCU) to interface between the camera and VCR. With portable recorders, the camera (or CCU) plugs directly into the recorder, which can also be mated to a tuner/timer and perform like a tabletop VCR.

A separate power belt is one way to power your portable VCR when using it on-location.

RADIO FREQUENCY

A term you'll come across increasingly as you learn about and live with video is "RF output." RF stands for Radio Frequency, a kind of unseen and unheard carrier wave that is modulated with picture and sound information to enable signals to travel through the air-waves. A television signal is video + audio + RF. A standard electronics analogy is that video and audio are similar to riders on horseback, while RF is similar to the horse.

A broadcast program is received by your television set as a "radio frequency" signal, which is processed by the internal electronics of the TV set, to remove the "horse" and leave only the riders (video and audio). When other sources of video programming are to be fed into the TV, however, it is necessary to ensure that they are first converted into an RF signal, as the standard TV cannot receive pure video or audio information.

Home programming equipment such as videocassette recorders, videodisc players, video games, home computers, and the like have "RF modulators" built-in so that they can be used easily and instantly with conventional TV sets.

A discussion of RF would not be complete without noting that it does have an effect upon the quality of the original video and audio signals it converts to television signals. The difference in picture quality might not be noticeable to the average eye, but placed side-by-side, a direct video signal fed into a monitor will be sharper, clearer, brighter, and cleaner than the picture produced by an RF-converted signal.

When hooking up equipment to the TV, be aware that the term "RF" can be used interchangeably with Very High Frequency, "VHF," and Ultra High Frequency, "UHF." More about this later.

GOING RF-LESS

There are circumstances that allow you to forget about RF, so that you can derive optimum picture quality from your VCR as it is playing back through your television set.

As you will read in the section on how to connect your equipment, (chapter 2), standard home TV receivers have VHF antenna connectors on the rear panel. The VCR connects to the TV for playback through these terminals.

Some TV models, properly called "monitors," have additional features on their rear panels, similar to those found on professional video monitors used by TV studios. These special connectors include video and audio input terminals or jacks.

The VCR has output as well as input jacks for both video and audio. Connecting the VCR's video/audio outputs to the video/audio inputs of these specially designed home monitors lets you bypass completely the RF conversion process. The result is better picture quality (i.e., less video noise).

The continuing growth and popularity of home video equipment such as VCRs ensures that more and more monitors will feature direct inputs for video and audio signals, so RF can be eliminated except for normal television reception. Cable systems presently feed RF signals into your TV set. Eventually, these features will become standard on every TV, regardless of price or screen size.

VIDEOCASSETTES

As previously explained, videotape and film are highly dissimilar media for recording and producing images. Unlike film, videotape is not designated as color or black-and-white. Its reproduction of color depends upon where the image is coming from and through what kind of TV it is being viewed.

For example, a black-and-white camera will produce black-and-white pictures, regardless of whether the program is viewed on a color or a monochrome television set. A program broadcast in color will be recorded in color by a VCR. It will play back in color on a color TV, but of course will appear in black-and-white on a black-and-white TV. This also applies to using a color camera, which has become all but standard for home video use. In fact, finding a store that sells black-and-white video cameras is not easy, since few companies manufacture them.

Another major distinction is the methods inherent in film and video to turn a recorded or exposed image into a positive one ready to be viewed. As a photo-chemical medium, film requires chemical processing before the image is visible. Once exposed to light, film cannot be used again. Videotape is a magnetic medium, just like audiotape. It is not photo-(light)-sensitive, so that the time and money required by film processing are eliminated. An image re-corded on videotape can be played back instantly, without even re-moving the videocassette from the VCR. As with audiocassettes, videocassettes can also be erased and used to record again and again. Good-quality videocassettes can be used and reused many times in this way without visible deterioration in picture quality.

Cassette Size and Format. Home video is still a new field, with different designs competing openly on store shelves. Whereas film sizes are standardized to fit all different makes of cameras utilizing their sizes, videotape is not.

Videocassettes are categorized according to tape width, meas-ured in inches. Both quarter-inch and half-inch tape are used in home recording, so be sure you know what type of tape your VCR is designed to accept. Video cameras can be used with any size of videotape.

To complicate matters for the beginner, even within the same widths of videotape there are different types of cassette that are not interchangeable. The size of the cassette will vary, so a half-inch cassette in format "X" does not fit properly into a VCR de-signed for use with a half-inch cassette in format "Y."

If you have friends who use a VCR, check the specific format of their equipment. If there is a clear consensus, use the same format and you'll be able to exchange tapes to play on each other's VCRs. If the format you own is not compatible with your friend's, you'll have to visit them to see their recorded videocassette programs, or they'll have to bring their VCRs to you.

Fortunately, format restrictions apply much less severely to video cameras. Generally, any type of home video camera can be operated with any kind of home videocassette recorder. In certain cases, you may require adapters so that the camera's cable plugs properly into the VCR, but beyond that, cameras and VCRs do not share the incompatibility problem prevalent among video-cassettes and VCRs.

It would not be fair, however, to indicate that the situation is entirely rosy when crossing cameras and VCRs of differing makes and formats. You will, with proper adapters, always be able to record and play back a camera's signal. But you normally will lose some special functions of the camera. Playback through the camera (if it has an electronic viewfinder) may not be possible, the trigger switch on the camera that orders the VCR to record may not function properly, and so on. In other words, whenever possible, try not to cross formats and brands, or at the least, check to see how many functions you will lose before you do—especially if you are considering buying an adapter.

Videocassettes are priced according to the length of their recording time in minutes. The shortest tapes for home use run thirty minutes, and longer tapes can run for up to six hours continuously. In the near future, longer running times are expected. The length of time a cassette will record can be extended on VCRs with multiple-speed settings. Each VCR format has a standard speed, which represents optimum picture quality since this is also the fastest speed at which the VCR runs. The faster the speed at which the tape runs, the better the picture and sound quality during record and playback.

Slower speeds sacrifice varying degrees of picture and sound quality, depending on VCR make and model. However, they also extend the cassette's recording capability, often by two or three times the recording time available at the fastest standard speed.

VCR FEATURES AND FUNCTIONS
Most of the capabilities of the VCR have already been discussed, so let's round out the full range of operation by looking at other important features pertinent to home video production.

The soundtrack of a videocassette is recorded simultaneously whether taping "off-air" from another recorder, or with a camera (through its built-in or external microphone).

A different soundtrack can replace the original soundtrack by plugging a microphone or other sound source (i.e., the output of an audio tape recorder, hi-fi system, etc.) into the VCR's *AUDIO DUB* jack. While playing back a videocassette you can then record

You can determine how much time you'll get from a blank cassette by set-ting the VCR to one of one, two, or three speeds (depending on model). This speed control (VHS illustrated here) shows the most common designations: SP for standard play, the fastest speed for optimum picture quality; LP for long play, which doubles cassette time vs SP; and SLP, for super long play, which triples cassette time vs SP. Many new models offer two recording speeds but three playback speeds to accommodate cassettes recorded on earlier models.

new audio over the old track without erasing the video portion of the program.

If a VCR has two separate channels of audio, depending on the unit's exact features, it can record "sound with sound" or "sound on sound"—meaning that a new track can be added to the original without loss of the original. Some models are able to record in stereo and may be played back in stereo when appropriately connected to your stereo system.

During playback of a program, you can achieve a variety of special on-screen effects. Possibilities include stop action, single frame advance, variable slow motion, and fast action. A full-featured model will offer these playback speed variations in reverse as well as forward. A critical feature for longer recordings is a high-speed picture search in both directions. This lets you rapidly locate a specific scene or segment on the tape in a fraction of the normal "real-time" playback.

These special playback modes of operation are not accompanied by sound. The exception is a VCR that employs a technique called

VIDEOCASSETTE RECORDER FEATURES AND FUNCTIONS

Eject—releases VCR loading compartment in which cassette has been inserted, allowing user to easily remove cassette from machine; also releases loading compartment when user is ready to insert cassette into machine.

Rewind—reverses direction, at very high speed, to automatically rethread tape from take-up reel back onto feed reel so that you are ready to play back or record tape from the beginning; no visible on-screen image.

Stop—power supply remains on, but all other machine functions come to a halt until another function is activated.

Fast Forward—similar to rewind feature, only with tape moving at very high speed from beginning to end; no visible on-screen image.

Play—if tape has been recorded, this will let you watch the images on your TV screen.

Record—puts machine in mode to store picture and sound images from any source it is connected to, such as TV antenna, cable TV connection, color video camera, or another video recorder.

Audio Dub—lets you replace the existing soundtrack on a videocassette program with a new soundtrack, which may come from a live microphone, from a record, audiocassette player, or any other sound source that can be plugged into the VCR.

Pause—unlike *STOP* control, this does not cancel out other functions of machine but only temporarily holds them in check for a few minutes until *PAUSE* is released, reactivating the *PLAY* or *RECORD* controls; most commonly used to stop *RECORD* during commercial or any unwanted program segment, or to halt *PLAY* if you wish to stop viewing tape for a short while. *WARNING: DON'T USE PAUSE FOR MORE THAN FIVE MINUTES AT A TIME. FOR LONGER INTERVALS, PRESS STOP.*

VIDEOCASSETTE RECORDER FEATURES AND FUNCTIONS

Stop Action or Freeze Frame—let you hold one frame of image on the screen to study it in detail; some freeze frames, depending on machine model, are stable and sharp, while others may jitter and exhibit horizontal lines or bars across image.

Frame Advance—lets you move one frame at a time on screen; often this feature doubles as stop action. Each time you press it, the image will move one frame at a time.

Slow Motion—visible, on-screen picture that plays back at a fraction of the normal playback speed.

Search—lets you scan the images on a recorded videocassette at a higher speed than normal playback in order to quickly find a segment or scene on the tape; usually works in forward and reverse; visible, on-screen picture.

VCR/TV Program Select—puts VCR in proper mode to play back recorded videotape or to switch to normal broadcast or cable TV source.

Tape Counter with Memory—Three- or four-digit counter to give relative indication of what point tape has reached. If memory switch is turned on, with counter set to all zeros, tape will automatically stop at that point during rewind.

Tracking Control—corrects for certain picture problems that occur during playback of a videocassette recorded on a different machine.

Electronic Programmer—lets user program VCR for recording of different channels at different times on different days while unattended.

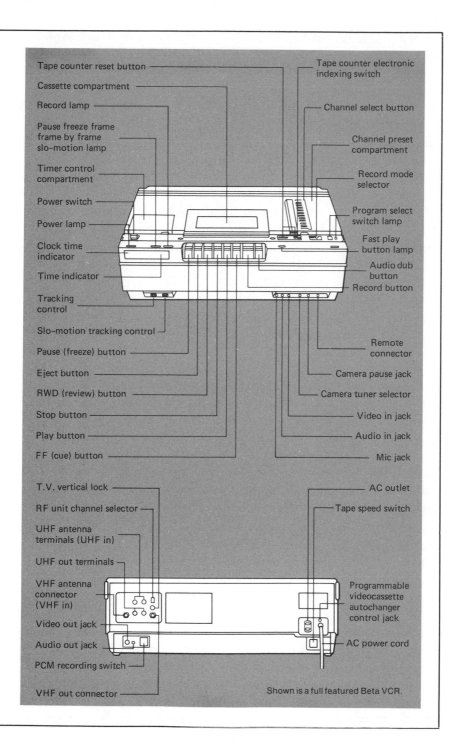

Tape counter reset button

Cassette compartment

Record lamp

Pause freeze frame frame by frame slo-motion lamp

Timer control compartment

Power switch

Power lamp

Clock time indicator

Time indicator

Tracking control

Slo-motion tracking control

Pause (freeze) button

Eject button

RWD (review) button

Stop button

Play button

FF (cue) button

Tape counter electronic indexing switch

Channel select button

Channel preset compartment

Record mode selector

Program select switch lamp

Fast play button lamp

Audio dub button

Record button

Remote connector

Camera pause jack

Camera tuner selector

Video in jack

Audio in jack

Mic jack

T.V. vertical lock

RF unit channel selector

UHF antenna terminals (UHF in)

UHF out terminals

VHF antenna connector (VHF in)

Video out jack

Audio out jack

PCM recording switch

VHF out connector

AC outlet

Tape speed switch

Programmable videocassette autochanger control jack

AC power cord

Shown is a full featured Beta VCR.

"voice compression" to retain an intelligible soundtrack even when the program is shown at two or three times its normal speed.

All VCRs have memory counters that display three or four digits. The counter looks like the mileage odometer of an automobile, except it doesn't actually measure any known quantity such as tape inches used or minutes of time. It is only a relative reference that indicates roughly what point the tape has reached as it measures revolutions of the take-up reel or the supply reel.

Effective use of this mechanical (or electronic) counter entails setting it to all zeros at the start of recording or playback. You can then note at what number a particular segment begins and ends and jot it down in a program log or on the label of the cassette involved. Before you begin recording a segment you can also set the counter at zero, turn on the memory and, during rewind, the cassette will automatically stop at the counter's zero setting.

Some VCRs have a form of electronic search that operates in fast forward. Typically, this feature works by allowing you to place an electronic signal at the beginning of each segment, or by sensing those small spaces between recordings where there are no images or sounds recorded.

On portable VCRs, an additional feature is the battery charge indicator that alerts you to how much power is available from your batteries and lets you know when it's time for a recharge.

Almost all of the VCR's features will be operable through a hand-held wired or wireless remote control. The price of the VCR reflects the degree of sophistication of its remote control. At a minimum, it is nice to have the search features controllable from the palm of your hand.

CAMERA FEATURES AND FUNCTIONS

The lenses supplied on home video cameras come in one of two basic configurations—fixed focal length or zoom. A zoom lens allows the user variable focal length as he or she zooms between wide-angle and telephoto settings. (The focal length of a lens is the distance between the optical center of the lens and the plane upon which the lens focuses the image it sees. In simple English, whether it is a wide-angle, a normal, or a telephoto lens.) For the serious video camera operator, the limitations of a fixed lens should become painfully obvious, and it should be eliminated from consideration when shopping for a camera.

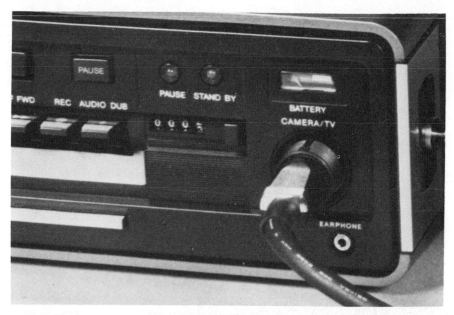

Portable VCRs have a mechanical digital counter, similiar to those on tabletop models, and also feature a battery-level indicator to alert the user as to how much battery power is left before recharging is required.

A VCR's remote control can save you a lot of wasted energy getting up from your chair. Pictured is a controller that offers the basic RECORD/ PLAYBACK functions (STOP, RECORD, PLAY, PAUSE) as well as special playback effects and the ability to change channels.

The speed of a lens is determined by the size of its aperture (iris) opening, and is measured in f numbers called "stops." (Lens speed refers to the amount of light a lens will pass to the camera. The faster the lens, the larger the opening and hence the less light will be needed.) Practically speaking, video cameras are supplied with lenses rated at $f/1.8$. Faster lenses are available down to about $f/1.4$ but will be far more costly for the small benefit of allowing you to shoot in lower light situations.

The lens assembly on a camera also has a focusing ring, zoom control (manual or motorized), and aperture (iris) control (automatic or manual).

The second most important component of the video camera in determining its versatility—and to a degree the quality of your production—is the kind of viewfinder employed. This is the eyepiece through which you view the subject area as it is seen by the camera's lens.

The optical through-the-lens (TTL) viewfinder is commonly found on basic cameras, with some exceptions, while the full-featured models offer electronic viewfinders.

Through-the-lens viewfinders are built into the body of the camera and do not offer instant playback of recorded material—a valuable feature of the electronic viewfinder.

The electronic viewfinder is actually a small (1.5-inch diagonal) black-and-white TV screen through which you view the scene your video camera sees exactly as it will appear on your TV screen during playback. Because it does not have to be housed within the camera body, most are made to be adjustable for the ideal viewing angle relative to the camera's position. This way you don't always have to twist and turn your neck to catch an unusual shot.

Some TTL models let you add an electronic viewfinder some time after purchase, but many are not so accommodating. Again, if your budget allows, choosing an electronic viewfinder for its convenience and flexibility will speed along your handling of the camera and minimize reshoots during production.

Viewfinders offer, in various combinations, a number of indicators to keep you constantly alert to all important camera conditions (light levels, on/off, battery power, etc.) without having to move your eye or head from the shooting position, thereby precluding the interruption of a shot.

You'll find certain camera features more critical than others in affecting the picture quality of your recordings. These appear on different models in varying combinations, depending on the price of the camera.

Auto/Manual Aperture (Iris) Control adjusts the amount of light entering the camera through the lens. Leaving the iris control set to its automatic position will prove ideal for most shooting situations except those in which you are trying to achieve an unusual or special effect. For these situations or where backlighting is a problem, a manual setting will be preferred.

White Balance. Each time you begin to record in a new lighting condition, this control should be used. Focusing on a bright, purely white object within view, you can adjust the setting so that all colors are reproduced accurately relative to the white object under illumination.

Color Temperature optimizes the camera for the ambient-lighting condition under which you are shooting. The white balance control, mentioned above, is actually a fine-tuning control for the color temperature setting. The control will be set to: sunlight, cloudy bright, tungsten, or fluorescent light, depending on your primary source of light.

Other camera controls that are not integral to operation but provide a more stylish, polished look to your production include:

Automatic Fade provides fades to and from "black" during camera recording for smoother, more professional transitions between scenes.

Backlight Control adjusts the camera's sensitivity to unusual lighting conditions, such as when the subject is illuminated from behind. It can also be used to experiment with special effects.

Macro Focus is a special feature of some zoom lenses. A macro adjustment allows you to lock the zoom ring into position for extreme closeup photography. The lens can then be focused on an object from a fraction of an inch to several inches away, depending on the lens model. This feature is ideal for videotaping documents, stamp and coin collections, and so forth.

*A camera with an electronic viewfinder (top) is ideal for serious video-
graphers, as it offers features and performance not available on cameras
with any other type of viewfinder. The electronic viewfinder is a 1.5-inch
(diagonal) black-and-white TV screen that displays the video image so
you can instantly monitor, in the camera, what you are recording, or play
back what you have just recorded. A few play back audio as well as video.
Most electronic viewfinders can be positioned for your comfort because
they are adjustable about the camera body. The through-the-lens type of
viewfinder (bottom) is more compact, built into the camera body, and lets
you view the scene exactly as it will appear on your screen. It cannot be
repositioned. It is possible with some TTL cameras to later add on an
electronic viewfinder.*

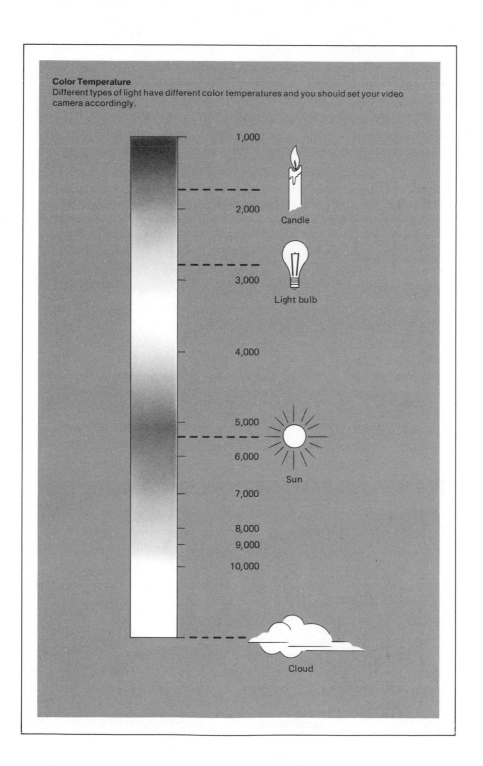

Color Temperature
Different types of light have different color temperatures and you should set your video camera accordingly.

1,000

2,000
Candle

3,000
Light bulb

4,000

5,000

6,000
Sun

7,000

8,000
9,000

10,000

Cloud

Interchangeable Lenses. Some cameras come with C-mount lenses. This designation indicates that the lens is removable and that any other C-mount lens may be interchanged with it. After mastering camera basics, you'll find filters and adapters available in camera specialty and supply stores to fit your lens and camera. These lens attachments broaden the range of "looks" your production can have, from atmospheric tints to dramatic starburst effects and much more.

Remote Controls. Almost all cameras have a VCR *PAUSE* switch to momentarily stop the tape as you move into position for another angle or adjust camera controls. Some models have more elaborate remote capabilities, including *RECORD* and *PLAY-BACK*, forward and reverse picture search, and frame advance. An optional accessory, this frame advance feature affords more "in-camera" editing flexibility and can save time and energy later on when you're involved in "editing" your tape during post-production.

Camera Sound. The microphone is a key camera feature. Most cameras have built-in mics, but their placement is critical to the sound quality of your program during playback. If the microphone is positioned too close to the lens, for example, such operating noises as the zoom lens motor will be picked up during recording.

The best configuration is a unidirectional boom microphone that extends at an upward angle from the top of the camera. Unidirectional mics concentrate on hearing sounds that come to them from one direction—in this case, in front of the camera. Omnidirectional mics, by way of comparison, pick up sounds coming from all directions. These sounds may include your hand making adjustments to the camera, airplanes passing overhead, or traffic and wind noises. A foam-rubber windscreen placed over the microphone significantly reduces the whistling sound of wind often heard in outdoor audio and video recordings.

The Hand Grip on the camera can extend straight down or angle toward the front or the rear. The grip should be removable, allowing you to attach special shoulder mounts and belly pods. On most quality cameras, removing the grip will reveal a mounting screw socket that allows the camera to be secured firmly to a tripod or other suitable support.

The best type of built-in microphone is a boom mic (pictured) that extends up and away from the camera. This design eliminates most noises due to camera handling or those coming from behind the person operating the camera.

Accessory Shoe. Finally, a well-equipped camera should have an "accessory shoe." This is similar to the "hot shoe" used on many still cameras to accept an electronic flash. On the video camera it can accept a small quartz lamp or external microphone.

ACCESSORIES

Acquainting yourself with available video equipment and accessories, even though it's before you're prepared to make full use of them, will round out your video knowledge and apprise you of what production possibilities exist.

A Tripod (for camera work) is absolutely necessary. Unless you want to give your audiences headaches from watching unsteady, dizzying results from a shaky hand-held camera, invest early on in a tripod and plan to put it to full use. Although a tripod may partially limit camera mobility, an overabundance of camera movement—as opposed to action taking place in front of the camera—is not a suggested technique. Moreover, dollies are available as accessories, allowing you to move both the tripod and attached camera around on three sets of wheels either during or between recording of scenes.

The tripod's head, upon which the camera sits, and its legs should be fully adjustable for angle and height. Try not to skimp by buying a very inexpensive tripod. You'll pay for it later when you notice it wobbling and unable to adequately support the camera as you tilt it (up-and-down angled movement) and pan with it (a lateral, side-to-side movement) during production.

Camera Extension Cables let you move farther away from the VCR, lessening interruptions and lengthening the continuity of a single scene without moving the VCR. The fewer editing cuts required during production, the better the finished result will appear once it's played back on the screen.

Adapter Cables may be needed if your video camera and VCR are made by different companies and are not immediately compatible. The connection at the end of the camera cable contains either ten pins or fourteen pins, depending on who manufactured it. Similarly, the camera input jack on the VCR may be either a ten-pin or fourteen-pin connector.

A Telecine Converter is a device used to transfer films and slides to videotape. A simple optical system, the unit takes a projected image and reflects it onto a small screen so that it may be recorded by the video camera with as little flicker as possible while still maintaining contrast and clarity. The color controls on the camera may be used during this process to enhance the look of the original films or slides.

Other accessories, some of which have already been mentioned in passing, include: AC adapters for portable VCRs and for camera connections to some tabletop, nonportable recorders; back-up battery packs for extended recording time in the field; portable VCR carrying cases and camera carrying cases; external microphones (and attachments), and camera lens attachments.

A simple optical device called a telecine converter lets you transfer home movies or slides to videocassette for improved preservation and for added convenience in viewing. The converter is placed between the film projector and video camera, reflecting the film image so it can be recorded by the camera onto a cassette.

BUYING TIPS

In explaining the features and functions of basic home video components, we have in most cases indicated what aspects are important to the budding videographer and for what reasons.

We've purposely avoided recommending, or even mentioning, particular brand names or specific formats, since individual preferences often differ. Quality, performance, and price will all have a bearing on the brand and format you select. However, these aspects and technology are forever changing and (with the exception of price) being refined. Therefore we have concentrated on the features common to all videotape equipment, and what they do.

Still, there are time-tested methods of equipment shopping that will help ensure that you don't waste precious dollars on a system you can't easily have repaired or grow disillusioned with due to lackluster performances or a lack of desirable features.

It's usually better to educate yourself properly before stepping out to comparison shop in stores. Product literature is usually available from the manufacturers directly, or from local shops, and even through specialty video magazines. Advertisers, in these and other related periodicals, make product information directly available to readers who can mail in a special card that is bound into the magazine. (Usually the reader circles numbers that specify which product the reader would like to receive information about.)

Perusing advertisements and articles in these publications will also educate you as to what equipment and features are available. However, major companies almost never include price in national advertising. Store owners do, however, state their prices in newspapers and in other forms of local advertising.

After you have first, determined what primary applications your home video equipment will be used for, you'll be able to decide which features are most important for your video system. An elementary example: if you're only interested in viewing prerecorded tapes and in recording programs one day at a time, you may as well purchase the most simple, lowest-priced videocassette recorder you can find. The added dollars you would spend for additional features you don't intend to use would be virtually thrown away.

In VCRs, extended programmability and electronic "push button" (solenoid) controls for recording and playback functions add to the price. Likewise, electronic push-button channel selection costs more than standard rotary dial tuning. Electronic or solenoid controls are quicker and more precise, are less prone to wear out from old age and equipment use, and offer dividends in machine operation that mechanical controls do not.

Case in point: Many mechanical models require you first to press *STOP* before going into another mode of operation. Most electronic or solenoid machines allow you to go directly from *PLAY* into *RECORD* or *FAST FORWARD*, etc. This feature proves its value when adding a scene to an existing tape with minimal visual interruption between two segments. This is a basic form of a production procedure called "assemble editing."

The most common and frequently lamented mistake that many first-time home video shoppers make is allowing price alone to determine the store they patronize. Many people simply go where they think they can get the best "deal."

With electronic equipment as complex as home video gear, you should ensure that your place of purchase is well equipped to provide professional servicing and carries a full line of accessories and other products you'll be needing as you learn more about your equipment and its potential.

Don't be misled by super discount houses featuring eye-grabbing low prices. All too often, this kind of dealer is not at all prepared to repair the products you've bought. Some will not even provide an over-the-counter exchange for products you've just purchased but which were faulty when you got them home. Also, most often, the salespeople are barely acquainted with the equipment and its features and will be of little or no help to you in making an informed purchase decision. They may even lead you to an entirely wrong purchase based strictly on price.

Specialty electronics or home entertainment shops, camera supply dealers, and reputable department stores may all be recommended. A good way to check out a store is to prepare a few basic questions to ask of a salesperson. Some questions that you might ask could be about the machine's programmability, its special playback effects, and how much cost electronic tuning adds. It won't take long to determine if the individual waiting on you is knowledgeable and can be trusted to offer you sound advice, or if the salesperson is an "order-taker" who can't tell you anything about the product that you don't already know.

As a note to first-time buyers, don't be afraid to have a salesperson compare and demonstrate different brands of equipment

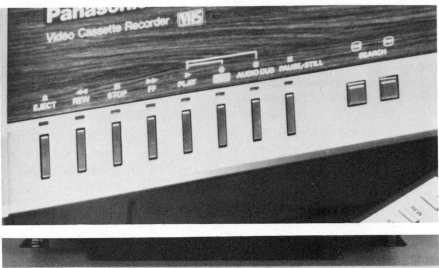

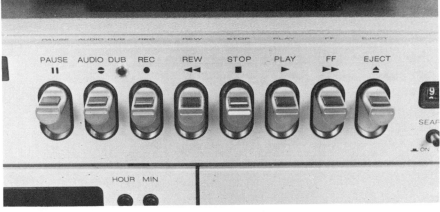

Electronic, "soft-touch" transport controls (top) are found on more expensive VCRs, while the lever-type mechanical controls (bottom) are more common on basic and older VCR models. Electronic push button controls offer more reliability and accuracy and save time in switching from one mode to another. Most importantly, they make possible wireless remote control operation.

for you. If you're unsure about two VCRs or cameras because they have similar features at identical prices, judge their relative performance and decide on that basis.

If the salesperson seems to grow exasperated at your request for demonstrations, pay no attention. It's your money. If you feel as though you are being pressured into buying something you're not fully satisfied with, take your business elsewhere.

At the time of purchase, it's always smart to make sure the store is giving you a factory-sealed carton. If it's not, ask why it has been opened and inspect its contents to be sure the equipment is new and in perfect condition. Also be sure that the package contains the manufacturer's warranty, along with all the other parts and paraphernalia you expect it to include.

Shopping in a reputable outlet also means the salesperson will see to it that you have any incidental items you need, such as a camera cable adapter or a battery if one is not included in the purchase price of a portable VCR. There is nothing more frustrating than the commonly shared experience of eagerly setting up a new home video system only to find you don't have some small but necessary item. This precaution includes having enough blank tape to record on when you leave the store.

Mail-order buying can be a smart way to purchase only if you have seen the product you are ordering in action at a friend's or a store, and you are thoroughly familiar with the model and all of its features. Also be sure the mail-order firm offers some kind of moneyback guarantee and it insures the goods while they are in transit for damages that may occur in handling and shipping.

INDUSTRIAL EQUIPMENT

No book on home video would be complete without some discussion of industrial video equipment. In terms of cost, the low end of the industrial spectrum covers the high end of the consumer market. However, in terms of features and performance there are cases where industrial products provide greater *value* to home video users than do their consumer counterparts.

Both Beta and VHS format VCRs are available in industrial models. Industrial Beta equipment runs at the one-hour Beta I speed only, a major disadvantage to the home user. All VHS machines, however, run at the standard two-hour playing speed, whether they are industrial or consumer models, and some industrial VHS machines offer the extended-play (four-hour and six-hour) speeds as well.

Industrial ½-inch VCRs are marketed primarily by Sony, Panasonic, and JVC. In their industrial lines, these manufacturers offer features consumers have been requesting for years. Stereo recording capability, while just beginning to creep into some consumer models, has been a staple of industrial equipment for years.

Frame-by-frame access, manually controlled audio recording, and built-in mic mixing are among the features available to industry but not yet to consumers. The big surprise is that, you may find that by carefully shopping, industrial decks with these features cost no more than top-of-the-line consumer models.

Industrial video cameras are also usually sturdier and vastly more flexible than their consumer counterparts. A feature such as Genlock (which is critical to multi-camera work) is only available on industrial or broadcast quality equipment. Genlock allows an external signal source to control those aspects of the camera that affect picture stabilization. If you are shooting with two or more cameras, they *must* be synchronized to each other by a Genlock signal. Otherwise, picture rolling, similar to that which occurs when you change TV channels too quickly, will happen most of the time as you switch from one camera to the other.

Portable industrial equipment is also built to take more abuse in the field and generally accepts a greater range of accessories and, in the case of video cameras, a greater range of lenses as well. However, this is not true of every single industrial product ever made. In fact, a few industrial models, particularly the lowest cost items in a line, are virtually identical to their consumer twins, except for the color of their cabinets or cases. This situation is changing, however, as ½-inch becomes the standard videotape format of industrial users.

If you are still wondering why you should consider industrial equipment, it is because for a relatively small increase in cost (and sometimes at no increase at all) industrial gear usually provides the finest quality picture and sound that Beta and VHS formats can deliver. If on-screen picture quality is a top priority for you, it will almost always be found in state-of-the-art industrial products.

Besides performance, there are other factors to consider. All industrial products carry a lengthy, meaningful listing of performance specifications—and the equipment must meet these specifications. Manufacturers do not usually provide much information concerning performance parameters on consumer models, and if they do, they will not always guarantee to meet them as published. With industrial gear you really know exactly what you are getting and that the equipment will perform as expected. This is not to say that consumer products will fall short of the mark, but only to emphasize that industrial products must meet it.

Industrial gear, at present, also affords its users a more modular approach to video than does consumer equipment. Because of the different design intention, industrial tuners, timers, power supplies, and specialized search and remote controls are sold separately from the primary tape transport mechanism.

Color video cameras usually feature sturdier, more advanced Vidicon tubes (called Saticons, Newvicons, or Plumbicons, etc.), interchangeable lenses, viewfinders, hand grips or shoulder mounts, mic configurations, and power sources. This benefits the buyer by ending built-in obsolescence. If a better viewfinder is needed, or a camera must be used for both field and studio work, the interchangeable features of industrial cameras provide a definite advantage.

Often accessories that are sold separately when you purchase consumer models come packaged with industrial equipment. For example, an expensive carrying case is usually included in the purchase price of a portable industrial VCR. Also, AC power supplies are frequently sold with industrial portables but are only available as accessories in the consumer marketplace.

Industrial warranties are usually much longer than consumer warranties, they generally cover both parts and labor for a one-year period. In addition, all AC-powered industrial equipment is Underwriters Laboratories (UL) commercial listed. Commercial listing is valuable for the business person whose video equipment is found to have caused a fire. This highly unlikely event, if caused by consumer gear that is only UL listed, may enable an insurance company to dishonor a seemingly rightful claim. For the consumer, commercial three-prong (grounded) equipment is marginally safer to use than the standard two-prong non-grounded variety. (But this is not to infer that consumer gear is in any way unsafe. It is almost totally without problems if used according to instructions. The grounded industrial approach merely gives the user a slight edge in safety.)

For most people our advice is to shop for and purchase consumer video equipment. But, if you think you will advance to more sophisticated usage in the near future, you should seriously consider industrial equipment. Should you wish to purchase industrial equipment, we recommend that you contact the industrial-division headquarters of the manufacturers mentioned previously. These companies are well staffed and equipped to answer any and all questions, even from consumers, and have sales materials and brochures that will make your choice easier and more pleasant.

One final note. If you are going to buy, or if at some time you decide to buy, industrial equipment, many dealers who sell consumer gear will be happy to get it for you at substantial savings. Industrial and broadcast outlets tend to charge list price for everything. For a company, school, or institution, the added cost is worth the advice and applications help the specialist firms offer. For the consumer who knows precisely what he or she wants, these extra services are probably not necessary.

The Panasonic model NV-8410 is a good example of low-end industrial equipment. The basic unit (shown here) comes with a sturdy carrying case.

2

INSTALLATION
AND OPERATION

When you set up video gear for the first time, the most important thing to keep in mind is that the process is really very simple. Even though the equipment may be all new to you, it won't be long before the thrill of controlling your own television programming is a reality.

A lifetime of familiarity with television, a little logic, this book, and your owner's manual will make you a "video pro" in a very short time.

It cannot be stressed often enough that you should take the time to thoroughly read your owner's manual. Although not always written in the clearest language, most manuals explain enough of the basics with sufficient clarity to allow you to operate your new equipment soon after you open the box.

In home video there are two essential components—the television set and the videocassette recorder. Without the VCR you have television, not video. Without the television set you have video—but no way to see it. Remember, a VCR records television signals from an antenna (or cable), etc., not from a television set.

To begin your installation, first decide where you want to place your VCR for maximum ease of use, safety (if there are small children in your household), and eye appeal.

In most cases placement will be on top of your television set (if it's a console model) or near it. Do not place it on top of the TV if your set gets hot during use. Remember that a VCR may be used as a remote channel tuner for your television set, so consider placing it near your favorite easy chair or sofa.

The VCR requires two sources of input to operate. One is 120-

volt AC power, the other is a signal from an antenna, cable TV system, video camera, or other video source.

The initial steps of installation, therefore, are to:

Find a suitable location for the VCR

Plug it into a wall outlet

Connect it to an antenna or cable system

ANTENNA CONNECTIONS

To connect your VCR to an antenna, follow the VCR manufacturer's instructions, which will identify the proper input connectors on the back panel of the VCR. In most cases you will find a 75 Ohm "f" connector input terminal. This terminal provides VHF channel (2–13) input to the VCR. Two screw-type terminals will also be provided for UHF channel input.

As a rule it is preferable to run all antenna wiring as close to the walls of your house as possible. It is also a good idea to use 75 Ohm coaxial cable for these runs. This type of wire is about a quarter-

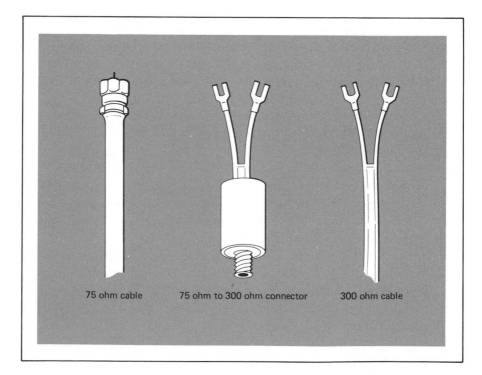

| 75 ohm cable | 75 ohm to 300 ohm connector | 300 ohm cable |

inch thick and round. You are probably more familiar with the 300 Ohm twin-lead wiring, which is flat and about a half-inch wide. Until recently it was used as standard wiring for most TV and FM radio antennas.

Coaxial cable (round) is preferred because it prevents the antenna leads from picking up stray television signals, which are always present in the air and may degrade picture quality. This is why video equipment is designed to use coaxial cable rather than traditional twin-lead wiring. However, reception of stray UHF signals is not considered much of a problem, and therefore UHF wiring is normally twin-lead, not coaxial cable.

If you have twin-lead wiring and do not wish to switch to coaxial cable, you will need a matching transformer, called a "balun," to make the antenna connection to the VHF *IN*put of your VCR in most cases. While many VCRs are supplied with baluns as an accessory, some may still come without one. In that case you can pick one up at any radio or TV store for a very modest price.

The antenna connections of your VCR will be marked *VHF IN* and *UHF IN*. The "*IN*" refers to *IN*put. These inputs are used to provide the VCR with almost all forms of incoming broadcast signals including antenna, cable, video games, videodisc, and signals from some home computers. This input is not used for video cameras, however—more on this later.

Therefore, the primary antenna connections to the VCR are the *VHF IN* and *UHF IN* jacks. Cable wiring will connect directly to them, twin-lead will require (in most cases) a balun (matching transformer) to provide VHF signal input.

If you also wish to utilize the full UHF capabilities of your equipment, the twin-lead or cable wiring of your antenna system must first be split (into VHF and UHF outputs) before it is connected to the *VHF* and *UHF IN*put terminals of the VCR.

> *Note*: Some splitters contain their own baluns and will take a twin-lead input and transform it into a twin-lead output (for UHF) and a 75 Ohm output for VHF—very handy and very inexpensive. If you purchase such a splitter, connection of twin-lead antenna wiring is simplicity itself.

If you take our advice and use 75 Ohm cable, then a similar splitter with a 75 Ohm (not twin-lead) input is required to bring both VHF and UHF channels into your VCR.

This may sound complicated but it is not, and the illustrations provided in this book and your instruction manuals should simplify the setting up of proper connections to your VCR.

CONNECTIONS TO YOUR TELEVISION SET

Having connected your antenna to the VCR, the next step is to connect the VCR to your television set.

The *VHF OUT*put jack is designed to be used with a 75 Ohm coaxial cable. For this connection twin-lead cannot be used—cable must be used.

If you have located the VCR at, or near, your TV set, then there is no problem. Most VCR manufacturers supply short connecting cables with their products. If you have placed the VCR some distance from the television set, then you must buy a special cable in the length you will need. All video shops, most major electronics stores, appliance shops, and department stores with video departments sell cables in various lengths.

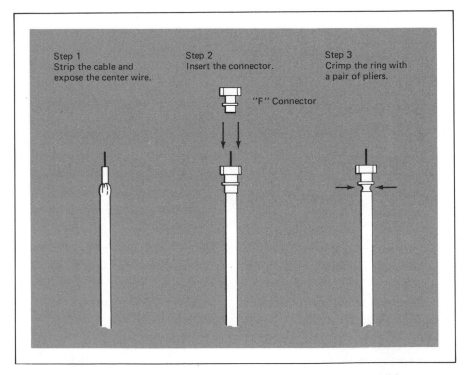

The correct means for attaching an "f" connector to 75 ohm cable.

If a very long cable is needed, your best bet is to have a video store make up a cable for you. Standard lengths are available up to 25 feet (7.6 m), and may, with a cable connector (barrel) be increased to 50 feet (15.2m). Remember, however, that the longer the cable, the weaker the signal from the VCR to the TV. Under 25 feet there should be no problem, but for extralong cables, a small TV signal amplifier may be needed.

The prepared cables you can buy come with "f" connectors on each end that are simply screwed onto the terminals of your VCR and TV set or are placed over these connectors. For permanent installations, the screw-on type of connector is preferred for its additional strength at the point of connection.

Some VCRs convert UHF channels to their VHF channel *OUT*-puts, some do not. For those VCRs that will not relay UHF signals to the TV set through their VHF *OUT*put terminals, a second cable or wire may be needed. This connection (because it contains only UHF signals) should be of 300 Ohm twin-lead wiring. It will allow you to watch UHF channels on your television set, normally, without having to power up your VCR in order to make a conversion to UHF.

All VCRs will convert UHF signals to a VHF signal when they are placed in their *RECORD* mode of operation. This means that you can run a single cable from the VCR's VHF *OUT*put to your television set's VHF *IN*put and, by placing your VCR in *RECORD*, use the VCR as an all-channel remote control tuner. If you require total independence of your TV set from your VCR, you will in some cases have to run duplicate wiring to the television set. The TV may then be operated normally when the VCR is not in use. This duplicate wiring is for UHF reception only, as all VCRs have a switch that passes the VHF signal straight through the machine.

A FEW WORDS ABOUT ANTENNAS AND CABLES
In home video it is crucial to maintain and produce the best possible images on a TV screen. After all, who wants to own or show poor-quality programs or movies over and over again? When programs were viewed only once, signal quality was not a paramount issue. We accepted poor-quality signals more readily and tended to watch TV more casually. If the signal wasn't "clear," we could, and did, live with it. Now, along comes home video and suddenly,

signal quality becomes very important. People are becoming accustomed to better-quality pictures on their TV sets. Movies on videocassette, videodisc, and cable TV have quickly educated us to the benefits of pictures we can see clearly.

With VCR ownership, marginally acceptable signals can easily become an ongoing annoyance. To record a program and be continually bothered by snow, ghosts, noise, and the like is unnecessary, if not downright aggravating. Certainly, cable TV is helping the situation. For those who have "cable" or can get cable, please ensure that your signal is as good as the cable company can make it. Do not accept poor reception on any channels. Cable promises excellent reception of all channels, especially "pay" channels—and that excellent level of reception should be yours.

For those who must rely on their own antenna, rabbit ears or more exotic indoor antennas are unacceptable. They simply cannot (except in the rarest of cases) supply your VCR with a good to excellent signal.

Outdoor antennas, installed years ago, or newer installations using twin-lead wiring, introduce ghost problems by picking up stray signals along the paths of their wires. The answer is to have the antenna rewired with 75 Ohm cable—in effect, creating your own cable system.

Therefore, for maximum enjoyment of your video investment, an excellent antenna or cable TV system should be used to provide signals to your VCR. Do not sell your equipment short by using inferior or substandard antennas or wiring, or drive yourself crazy by "making do" with an indoor antenna that requires constant adjustments and reacts to the vagaries of atmospheric conditions.

BASIC OPERATION OF THE VCR

Videocassette recorders come in two basic configurations: the more common console (home) models and portables. Both styles of machine perform the same basic functions (more or less). The portable VCR separates the functions that are found in the console model into two self-contained units. One is the tuner/timer and the other is the basic record/play tape transport. Because of this portables are not merely lightweight versions of home VCRs.

Basically VCRs are little more than glorified tape recorders, similar to audio tape recorders. Many of their controls are similar.

A VCR differs from an audio tape deck in that its features permit not only recording and playback, but also the selection of the material to be taped (through its tuner section) and also the time of day (and sometimes the day of week) that taping is to take place. In addition, many advanced VCRs contain circuits that allow them to perform electronic "tricks" with the tape (only in playback), such as "freeze frame" viewing, slow and fast forward and reverse while viewing, sound dubbing, cassette changing, and more. Notwithstanding these "tricks," the two necessary and most basic functions of the VCR are recording and playback of electronic signals.

Playback requires very little discussion. All machines work similarly in this aspect of their operation. The VCR must be plugged into a wall outlet. It must be properly connected to a television set or video monitor. A videocassette must be inserted into the machine. Then simply depress the *PLAYBACK* control.

Two final checks may be necessary the first time playback is attempted. First, that the VCR's output is operating on an unused channel in your area. (In the United States this will always be either channel 3 or channel 4.) Second, that the television set is fine-tuned to the channel on which the VCR is operating. (Locations of all controls necessary to operate the VCR in playback will be found in your instruction manual.)

The reason we mention all these rather obvious points is that many people have trouble the first time they operate their VCRs because they neglect one of the points enumerated. Like many procedures, it takes far longer to explain the playback function than to actually perform it.

Recording is a bit more complex. Most of today's VCRs utilize electronic tuning rather than the outdated, click-stop rotary tuning dial of yesteryear. In some cases these newer machines may require a modest bit of tuner programming to get things going. They all leave the factory properly tuned to the VHF channels 2 and 13, but to tune many of them to UHF channels requires active participation on the part of the owner. Whether your VCR can tune 110 or 14 channels, when you get beyond channel 13 you're often going to have to adjust the tuner. This of course does not apply if your tuner is factory preset for more than 13 channels. Some are made that way, some are not. Instructions for programming the tuner section of your VCR vary with each manufacturer's make and model. The instructions are usually posted on the machine at or near the door to the tuner control section. They are also found in the owner's manual that comes with the VCR. Therefore, if you have and wish to record UHF channels, or if you simply wish to program your VCR in a different way than it was supplied from the factory, please refer to your machine's individual tuning instructions. Once you have programmed, or accepted the machine's programming, your video recording can begin.

And, if you subscribe to cable TV, no programming at all should be necessary. The cable company's converter box will feed your VCR all channels, as selected by the tuning dial or pushbuttons on the converter. Simply tune your VCR to the channel the cable company uses (it is the same channel to which your TV set was tuned when you first got cable) and you're in business.

The next step is to ensure that the timer of your VCR is set accurately. Time tones broadcast by television and radio stations may be used for this purpose. If you live in a large city, the telephone company usually has a number to call for the exact time. This is probably the most accurate of all sources.

For those installations using an antenna, programming your VCR to tape desired broadcasts is now a simple matter. Your owner's manual will provide exact procedures for you to enter into the machine—channels, times, and dates. The VCR will do everything else.

People with cable TV systems that use a converter box have problems. There are two ways around the problems caused by cable company converters. The first is to have the cable company install an additional converter box, one for the TV, one for the VCR. However this solves only part of the problem. You can watch one program and record another, but you lose the ability of the VCR to record programs automatically on different channels. The second, and more satisfying solution is for you to install an "up" or "block" converter in place of the cable company's converter. The "up" converter is used to take all the channels coming through the cable and convert them to UHF channels that may be programmed, like any other UHF channels, into your VCR. If your cable company's converter box also contains a pay TV decoder, then that too may be routed into the system, restoring use of all cable channels to the VCR.

The only major problem of "up" conversion is that it may cause some confusion as to which channel numbers your local VHF TV stations will appear on. For example VHF channel 7 may be converted to UHF channel 63. A reference guide comes with each "up" converter but it will take some time getting used to the new channel number allocation caused by these devices. The "up" converters may be purchased at most video stores and stores with video departments. They are also available by mail order and all come with complete instructions for installation. Again, they are not complicated, they just sound that way. The converters can also be expensive.

If your VCR is "cable ready," then it already contains a built-in "up" converter. You will still need the cable company's converter if it contains a decoder for pay channels. The pay channel will be inputted to your VCR on an unused VHF channel in conjunction with the "up" converter. All other channels will appear on UHF frequencies. (If you are going to be home when you wish to record you may, of course, operate the tuner selection on your machine manually.)

Remember, because each VCR is programmed differently, refer to the owner's manual for the specifics of your particular machine. Also (we cannot state it often enough) check and double check all tuner/timer programming. Many a VCR owner has left home thinking all is well with the machine, only to return and find out: that the tape had never been loaded, or that the machine had never been set to tuner/timer operation. Or perhaps the tuner/timer had been misprogrammed or set for the wrong time of day. It may sound silly, but these things happen, even to the most experienced of users.

Another point worth remembering, especially with multispeed machines, is to be sure you've set the proper speed to allow enough taping time. Don't leave six hours of programming to be recorded, while you're on vacation, with the machine set to the two- or four-hour speed.

If all of these steps are followed, recording is as simple as actuating the record button(s) whenever you wish to record a program.

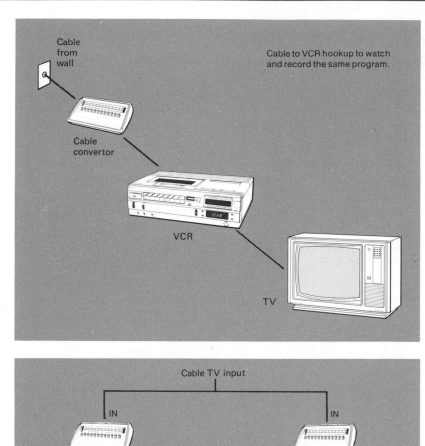

Cable
from
wall

Cable to VCR hookup to watch
and record the same program.

Cable
convertor

VCR

TV

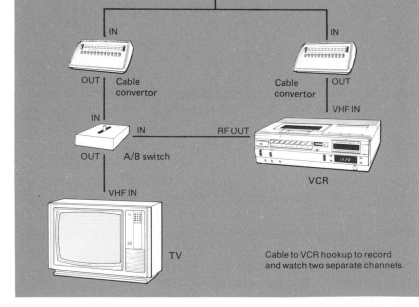

Cable TV input

IN

IN

OUT   Cable
      convertor

Cable   OUT
convertor

VHF IN

IN

IN   RF OUT

OUT   A/B switch

VCR

VHF IN

TV

Cable to VCR hookup to record
and watch two separate channels.

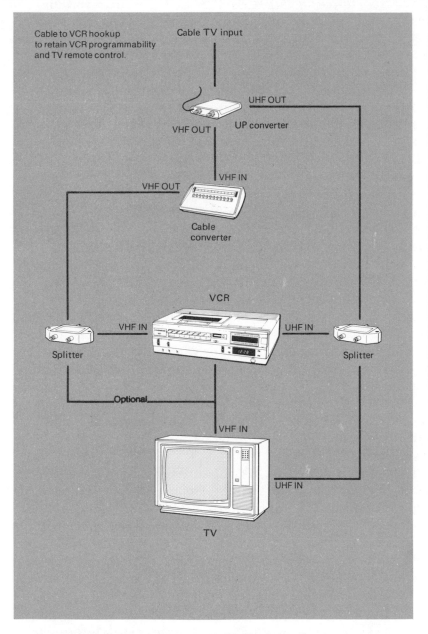

Cable to VCR hookup
to retain VCR programmability
and TV remote control.

Cable TV input

UHF OUT

VHF OUT   UP converter

VHF OUT   VHF IN

Cable
converter

VCR

Splitter   VHF IN   UHF IN   Splitter

Optional

VHF IN

UHF IN

TV

Illustrated are the three most often used cable TV wiring designs. As you can see, even
with a cable company converter box, full programmability and remote control functions
can be maintained with the proper use of video accessories.

The Importance Of Pause And Stop. If you are recording off-air (as opposed to duping from another videotape) you may wish to delete commercials or station breaks from your tape. This editing, like most half-inch video editing, is best done at the time the recording is being made. It cannot be accomplished while you are away from home and the recorder is operating automatically.

Although several companies produce equipment to eliminate commercials, these devices are not nearly perfect in their operation. Some commercials will creep through, some station breaks will be recorded and, worse yet, some of the programming you wish to record may be lost.

It is, therefore, always best to sit by the VCR and "nursemaid" the process of recording any program you wish to keep permanently. Only people, not machines, can make the proper judgments as to when to place the recorder in its *PAUSE* mode. And, if a mistake is made, there is usually time to correct it if the recording process is being monitored.

The mechanics of editing out unwanted programming are simple. The *PAUSE* control of your VCR places the machine in a "holding" situation. The tape is kept in proper position to resume recording—against the record heads within the machine—and the VCR's electronics are kept ready to instantly resume the recording function. *PAUSE* controls must be used judiciously, however. If the *PAUSE* condition is allowed to remain for more than just a few minutes, permanent damage to the tape or the record heads can occur because of the heat due to friction between the spinning record heads and the tape.

For this reason, most VCRs will automatically go from *PAUSE* to *STOP* if left in *PAUSE* too long. Some may even resume recording; however, a shift in function from *PAUSE* to record, playback, or stop, will occur automatically. This shift varies from machine to machine.

Regardless of tape format, the *PAUSE* control stops the recording (or *PLAYBACK*) process temporarily. It is different from the *STOP* function because, as mentioned, it holds the tape in place to resume function instantly, where as *STOP* is used for long pauses. In the *STOP* mode, tape tension against the VCR's internal parts is relieved, only the electronics of the machine are left energized. Therefore *STOP* should be used for long pauses, anything over a minute or two, while *PAUSE* is used in editing out short lengths of unwanted programming (such as commercials or station breaks).

THE USE OF ACCESSORIES

Earlier, we described many of the video accessories available to make your life with video more easygoing and pleasant. At this point, having installed your new equipment, and having a good idea of how to operate it, the need for accessories should be more obvious than ever.

As soon as video systems contain more than one television set or VCR, they begin to require switching devices. Even if you only have a single TV set, if you add a VCR and a video game, a video switch eliminates having to rewire each time you change the input to the TV.

The best switchers on the market are electronic switchers. Mechanical switchers, while they are useful, and some are even quite remarkable in the number of inputs and outputs they can handle, all suffer from problems of "crosstalk"—various TV signals actually mix with other TV signals within the switchers and cause various degrees of video distortion. There is also some loss of signal strength within the mechanical switchers, due to the many splitters used in their construction. The electronic switch eliminates these problems.

If you need no more than the ability to have your television set choose among three sources of input, an antenna or cable signal, a VCR, and a video game, then the simple A/B mechanical switch will be more than adequate. The antenna is connected to the VCR's input as described earlier. The output of the VCR is connected to one side (either A or B) of the switch. The other side of the switch is connected to the video game. The output (center connector) of the switch is connected to the TV set.

The result is that in switch position "A," for example, the TV set is connected to the VCR and operates normally. It can receive straight antenna or VCR signals. In the "B" position the TV set receives the output of the video game. Beyond this simple illustration, hookup arrangements become more complex. There is no shortcut to calculating how many inputs (signal sources) your system will contain, and then deciding to how many television sets these outputs will go.

If you have several TV sets and contemplate at least one VCR and perhaps a videodisc player, the wiring situation becomes more complicated and decisions will have to be made. There is no end to the number of pieces of equipment you can wire into your system. To do so will require additional wiring and switching devices.

A switcher is almost essential for interconnecting a number of different video compontents (such as a videodiscplayer, videogame, or home computer, etc.) to one or more TV sets or VCRs. A high-quality electronic switcher is shown above.

At this point, if you are having trouble understanding the basics of equipment connections, please refer to earlier pages in this chapter.

Video Accessories. Another area in which the manufacture of video accessories is proliferating is that of signal enhancers and stabilizers. These devices are made to help consumers make better copies of existing prerecorded videotapes. In some cases the stabilizers are necessary to enable playback of prerecorded tapes on older TV sets. This is because many prerecorded tapes contain a weakened stabilizing signal, strong enough to play properly on a TV set but so weak that a VCR has trouble recording it. The problem shows itself as the constant rolling of the picture. A stabilizer

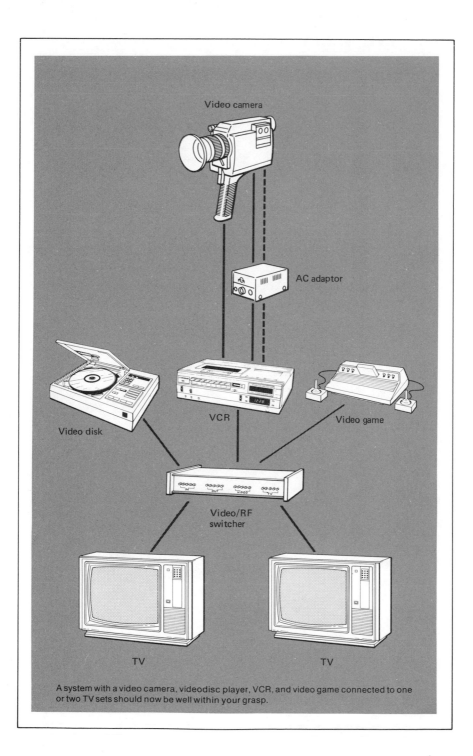

Video camera

AC adaptor

Video disk

VCR

Video game

Video/RF
switcher

TV

TV

A system with a video camera, videodisc player, VCR, and video game connected to one
or two TV sets should now be well within your grasp.

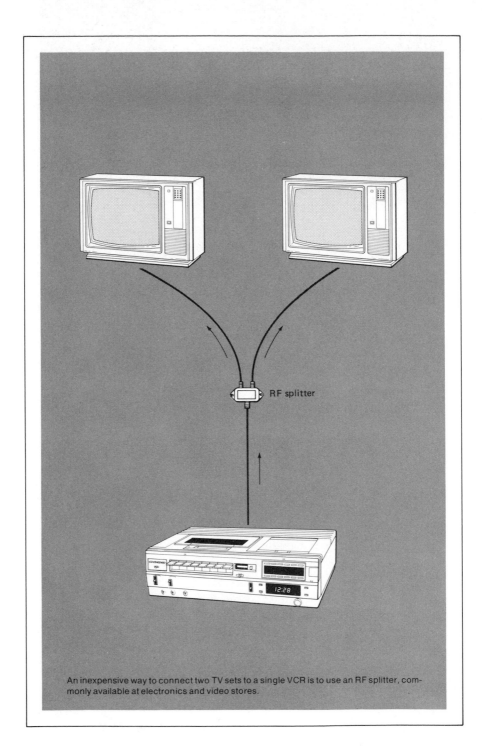

RF splitter

An inexpensive way to connect two TV sets to a single VCR is to use an RF splitter, commonly available at electronics and video stores.

eliminates the problem by regenerating the weakened signal and bringing it up to normal strength. Enhancers are signal shaping devices that, in some cases, help restore small portions of the video signal normally lost in the recording process. They can help make the picture sharper, clearer, and more colorful. Again, they are designed for tape-to-tape copying, not for enhancing signals from an antenna or cable TV connection. They may work on some antenna signals but are not worth their fairly high price unless you do a lot of duplicating from prerecorded tapes.

Other accessories worth mentioning are signal splitters. These are very inexpensive, small metal boxes having a single input connection on one end and two output connectors on the other. They are used, for instance, if your VCR must supply a signal to two television sets. You would then connect the output of the VCR to the input of the splitter. The output of the splitter would be connected to each of the two television sets you wished to use.

Additional accessories are available and many are non-electronic. There are devices to house videocassettes, video systems, and to protect your components. Electronic accessories include add-on remote controls, block converters for cable systems, and many other items.

At the point where your system requires the extensive use of accessories, you are already beyond the scope of this book and should seek professional help with your system or read other books written specifically for advanced videophiles.

3

THE HOME VIDEO PHOTOGRAPHER

After taping off-air for a while, or perhaps playing back prerecorded videocassettes, most people get the urge to create their own programming. And it is great fun to see yourself and your family on TV.

Connecting a video camera to a VCR can be simplicity itself. If your VCR is portable and will be used for frequent camera work, then in most cases only one cable need be connected to the VCR. If your camera is to be connected to a console VCR, you may need an adapter, which will plug into the wall and supply power to the camera. The camera will plug into the adapter and the adapter, through one or two built-in cables, will attach to the VCR.

If you are starting from scratch, buy a camera that was made to work with your specific VCR, unless you intend to upgrade the VCR at some future time. In that case buy the best camera you can and make do until you upgrade your VCR to match it.

Operation of the video camera is not at all difficult. After a few minutes it will become even easier than operating a super-8 movie camera. And if you have never operated a camera before, there is less to learn in video than there is in shooting film.

Video cameras come in all shapes, sizes, and prices. Their purpose is to gather light and sound and translate it into electronic signals for your VCR to record and television to play back.

All video cameras, whether black-and-white or color, perform this same function. But, unlike a film camera, you cannot switch between black-and-white and color by changing film or its video equivalent, videotape or the tube within the camera.

If you buy a color camera, you will always shoot in color but you may choose to watch the results in black-and-white by turning

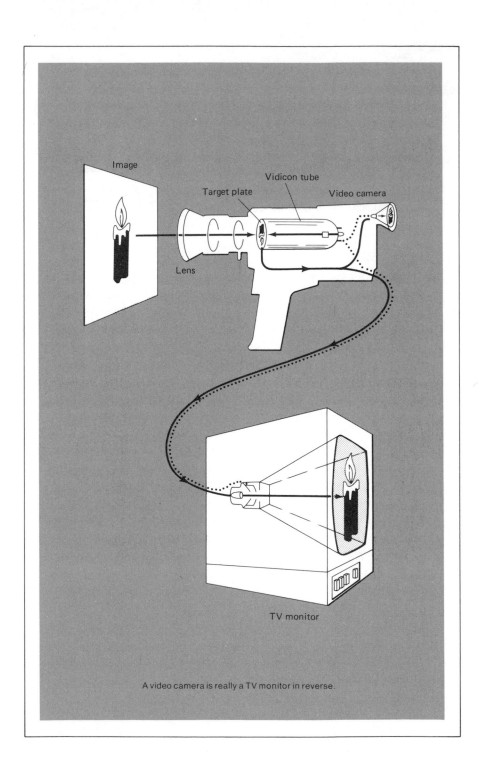

Image

Vidicon tube

Target plate

Video camera

Lens

TV monitor

A video camera is really a TV monitor in reverse.

If you are using a camera with a VCR that does not have direct camera input, you'll need a camera control unit (CCU), such as the one shown. The camera is connected to the CCU, which is then plugged into the VCR.

down the color control of your TV set or by watching on a black-and-white television. If you buy a black-and-white video camera, no color can ever be added.

The simple black-and-white camera shares many similarities with the color camera. Its lens must be focused, its aperture must be properly set, it looks and feels similar in use, and it can provide a signal for your VCR to record. That is, however, where the similarities end.

Color cameras shoot in color, cost a good deal more than black-and-white cameras, have many more special-effects features, and have controls to adjust the cameras to the various colors of ambient lighting. These latter controls are similar in performance to the kinds of filters that photographers use during indoor shooting or very early in the morning or late at night. In video they are called *color temperature* and *white balance* controls. Beyond controlling the differences in the qualities of ambient light, focusing and setting the aperture (iris), many color video cameras have special features. However, before we get into these features, some basics of photography must be discussed. If you already have a photographic background, all of this should be familiar to you.

THE LENS

The lens (usually a zoom) on a video camera is the optical assembly of the camera that actually gathers light—sees the picture. Its purpose is to take this light and focus it onto a device (the Vidicon tube) in the camera that (with the aid of electronic circuits) translates what it sees into an electronic video signal. If you were shooting with film, the lens would focus its light onto the film. There are two primary controls built into a lens. One is the focus control, the other is the aperture control.

In a zoom lens there is a third control called the *zoom ring*. This control is used to regulate the focal length (angle of view) of the lens. The focusing ring of the lens should, of course, be set to the distance between the camera and the subject being photographed. The aperture control determines the amount of light the lens will pass. Think of it as a "faucet" for controlling light. Too much light and the picture (or image) is overexposed. It will appear too light or all white. Too little light and the picture will be underexposed. It will look too dark or all black.

Note: Most video cameras contain automatic aperture controls that simplify exposure control considerably.

The zoom selector ring allows the camera operator the use of a lens that may be set from wide-angle to telephoto without the need to own and constantly switch several different kinds of lenses. That is why zooms are so popular among all kinds of photographers—still, movie, and video.

Some zoom lenses are motorized, some are not. The advantage of a motorized zoom is that it steadies the zooming process and makes it more uniform in speed. The disadvantages are greater cost, more weight, higher power consumption, and the prevention of manually selected zooming speeds for special effects. In some cases the motors used to actuate the zoom feature may actually be heard by the video camera's built-in microphone. For people who are not camera "nuts" the motorized zoom is usually preferred.

Some advanced cameras feature lens interchangeability, allow-

A video camera's telephoto lens may have three rings on it: the aperture ring (extreme right in photo) to control the size of the iris, which lets in light; the zoom ring to adjust the lens for close-up, wide-angle, and in-between focal lengths; and the focus ring (extreme left in photo).

ing the camera operator the option of selecting special-purpose lenses. Super-wide-angle and extreme telephoto are good examples. Interchangeability also allows the use of nonvideo lenses, such as those found on 35mm and movie cameras, with varying degrees of success. It's a nice feature, but not necessary for most people. Also keep in mind that the cost of additional lenses, especially those made specifically for video cameras, is considerably higher than their film camera equivalents. The situation gets worse if the accessory lens contains an automatic aperture control.

Most cameras that have automatic aperture controls provide a manual override control. This is a much preferred arrangement, as it allows you to compensate for any peculiar lighting conditions you may encounter, and more important, to fade in and fade out the image the camera sees. Other cameras have built-in fade controls for this purpose.

For those entering home video photography directly from still photography, a critical point to keep in mind is the difference between focal lengths in video lenses and on still camera lenses.

For example, at the wide-angle setting, an 11mm lens in video is the equivalent of a 40mm focal length in still photography. At the other end of the focal-length spectrum, a video camera's 45mm zoom compares with a still camera's 162mm telephoto setting.

THE "FEEL" OF THE CAMERA

The most important consideration in using a video camera is the way it feels in your hand and/or on your shoulder. Although video cameras weigh between three and eight pounds (1.4–3.6kg), it doesn't take long for a video camera to feel like it weighs a ton.

For this reason different designers have constructed their cameras in various shapes and sizes to provide the best and most comfortable designs. Sometimes their ideas of comfort do not match those of the end user—you. So it is important to physically try a video camera before you buy one.

Heft and feel are very important for the extended periods of shooting that video invites. Video productions invite longer shooting periods than does movie making. Therefore, do not use your experience with movie camera equipment as the basis for choosing your video camera.

CAMERA HANDLING: WORKING THE CONTROLS

Having first set up the video camera according to the manufacturer's directions, you are ready to begin shooting. Be sure the VCR is loaded with blank tape or tape you won't mind erasing. Be sure that all connecting cables are properly attached, and if you are using a console VCR, that the camera's AC adapter is plugged in and powered.

Since virtually all video cameras have an on/off trigger to pause the recorder, the VCR should be set to *RECORD* after the camera is attached and energized (turned on).

With console VCRs, particularly older models, recording may have to be controlled by the recorder, not by the camera. This is also necessary with portables that are not fully compatible with your camera. In that case the trigger on the camera will have no effect on the recording process and the camera should be regarded as a studio camera requiring the use of a studio engineer. In this case you are the engineer as well as the camera operator. It doesn't hurt to have an assistant if the camera cannot control the recording function. With all portables and many home VCRs, the camera will control recording and, for our purpose, we will assume that your combination does.

With the trigger operating properly, and the VCR set to *RECORD*, please keep two things in mind—that the camera's *OFF* command will place the recorder in the *PAUSE* mode, not in the *STOP* mode; and, that if the camera is used to halt the recorder for any appreciable length of time (more than a few minutes) the VCR will automatically switch to its *STOP* mode to protect both the tape and the recording heads in the VCR. This point is especially important if you are shooting in the field and are unable to keep a careful eye on your timing. The camera may not indicate that the VCR has automatically switched to *STOP* and you may continue shooting, thinking you are in *RECORD*. The rule is, use the trigger sparingly to start and stop recording from the camera. Double and triple check that the VCR is recording if any doubt at all exists. Make sure that the tally light is on and that the tape is moving.

If your camera does not have a trigger start/stop switch, it probably has this vital control situated elsewhere on its body. Wherever the location, it always performs the same function of pausing the deck when actuated in the *RECORD* mode.

THE VIEWFINDER
All video cameras feature one of three kinds of viewfinders to aid in focusing the camera and framing the subject properly. The more expensive cameras usually have what is called an electronic viewfinder. This is in reality a small 1½-inch (4cm) black-and-white television screen affixed to the camera body. Some electronic viewfinders are removable and very handy, while some are not.

Electronic viewfinders, used by all professionals, show you exactly what is being recorded by your VCR. It is in effect a miniature TV monitor. It also allows for very accurate focusing, especially if the camera is first zoomed in on the subject. The procedure: pause the VCR, zoom for maximum close-up, focus, zoom out for proper framing, shoot.

The viewfinder also allows you to check the tape you've made immediately, as the VCR may be played back through it.

Coming down a peg in performance, and quantum leaps away in terms of versatility, is the optical through-the-lens (TTL) viewfinder. This type of viewfinder is a carryover from movie photography that allows you to focus and frame as accurately as the electronic viewfinder, and in color, but does not allow actual monitoring of the recorded image or playback.

Lastly, some inexpensive, fixed-focus models will have an optical viewfinder. This device, simply a lens in a frame, allows you to aim your camera and nothing more. Since the camera is already focused, there is no point in providing any form of sophisticated viewfinder, and so the manufacturers have not done so.

COLOR TEMPERATURE/WHITE BALANCE
These controls or their variations apply only to color video cameras. They are used to obtain true colors under varying light conditions that may be present.

Remember from your photographic days how you had to set your movie camera for "indoor" or "sunlight." Or perhaps you had to buy "indoor" film or use a filter on your camera.

In video the selection of a filter or type of "film" is done electronically. The controls for achieving this filtration are similar to a color television's tint or hue control. With a camera these adjustments are made prior to shooting, not at the time you view the results. In fact they cannot be made after shooting, as the range of settings on a color TV will not correct for extreme color adjustment errors made in the field. Therefore the proper control of color temperature and white balance is critical for good-quality color video photography. The method and controls for setting the camera vary from model to model and by brands. Usually you simply have to turn a dial (for color temperature) to align a pointer on the dial to a scale showing pictures of the kind of light you are shooting in. Most cameras will adjust for sunlight, open shade, and tungsten or fluorescent light. The more deluxe camera will also have a white balance control. This is really a means of fine-tuning the color temperature adjustment even further. This control may have one or two dials to turn. It varies the level of *red* and *blue* intensity within the camera to assure that all colors will be recorded in proper balance to one another. If the white balance is set automatically, you simply have to point the camera at a white object (within the light conditions under which you will be shooting) and let the camera make the adjustment. If the setting is not automatic, you may choose to leave the controls set at their midpoints or adjust the controls until a metering device built into the camera indicates the proper setting. Under almost all circumstances, the preset color temperature control settings will be more than adequate. It is an added refinement to have a white balance control as well. Regardless, color temperature should be checked and possibly reset every time you change lighting conditions.

If a mixture of light is being used, say shooting indoors under room lights with sunlight streaming in from the windows, set the camera for the kind of light that predominates. Better yet, connect the VCR and camera to a color television set and adjust the TV set for a proper color picture on a broadcast channel. After switching to the VCR, you may use the TV set as a monitor for making the final color settings on the camera.

In the field you probably won't have a color monitor with you, so you have to rely on the basic camera settings for the kind of light you're shooting in. It will almost always yield an acceptable result, and after some experience with the camera, you will be able to make minor adjustments with the skill of an experienced camera operator.

PUTTING IT ALL TOGETHER

With focus and color temperature set, the only thing left to adjust before shooting is the aperture. Virtually all cameras have automatic aperture control. A few may require manual settings of this critical area. If you have a camera with only manual setting, there should be an exposure indicator either in the viewfinder or on the camera body. It is the equivalent of a photographer's light meter. The indicator should be set, and it varies by camera make and model, to the correct position as shown by a meter, lights in the viewfinder, or a scale printed on the side of the camera.

Once the aperture is set, the camera focused, color temperature adjusted, and the subject framed, you are ready to shoot. Remember, it takes a great deal longer to explain these adjustments than it does to make them.

Many of the newest cameras make so many settings for you automatically (focusing, aperture, white balance) that it should not be long before the "aim-and-shoot" video camera is common.

SOUND, LIGHTING, AND SET DESIGN

With the exception of microphone placement, most outdoor work will not entail any form of sound or set design or lighting control.

These aspects of video photography are relegated to indoor work and will be discussed shortly. Microphones, however, are something you have control of wherever you shoot video.

Sound. The microphones built into virtually all video cameras will suffice for most of the indoor and outdoor shooting you do. They are sensitive, able to reproduce all the audio frequencies the VCR can record, and require no special handling or attention. The only exception is to make sure the windscreen is attached on windy days when shooting outdoors.

Problems occur when miking an outdoor shoot if you are situated a great distance from your subject. The built-in mics will then pick up far less of the action and far more of the noises around the immediate camera position. For many people this will not be grossly objectionable, but for some people, and under certain circumstances, there may as well be no sound pickup at all.

The only solution is to use external microphones and place them on or near the subjects themselves, or else utilize "shotgun" mics.

The "shotgun" mic is a highly directional, physically elongated microphone that picks up sound from the direction in which it is aimed. It got its name from its rifle barrel appearance. It rejects almost all other sound and so may be used at great distances from the subject. But it requires constant "hands-on" aiming to function properly. This is the problem for the lone camera operator. Unless the video camera is on a tripod, operating by itself, one cannot control both the camera and the microphone and still attend the VCR with any degree of control.

If, on the other hand, a two-person crew can be arranged, the shotgun microphone solves the audio problems of long-distance camera work.

Shotgun mics are seen frequently at sporting events, are heavily used by the news media, and occasionally find themselves in the hands of home video enthusiasts. The shame is, there are few inexpensive models on the market.

Otherwise, a soundtrack made under quieter circumstances may be dubbed onto the final videotape production during post-production editing. In movie parlance this is called "looping."

Other than shotgun mics, almost any kind of microphone may be used with any VCR, or in some cases plugged directly into the camera. For interviews, at parties, social events, weddings, etc., it may be preferable to carry several small lavalier mics—the kind you see on people's lapels in TV broadcasts—and place them on subjects in advance of the camera work. A problem of working with several mics at one time is that they require a mixing device to bring their sounds together at the same volume level, and they may intimidate people who may otherwise be cooperative in your video venture.

Lighting for video begins with normal room lighting and extends to the use of several quartz lights to augment it. Few people realize that the lighting in a TV studio all but equals sunlight at noon in its intensity.

While many home video cameras will provide a viewable picture, under room lighting conditions, for full-color high-quality video, lighting has to be increased significantly to provide maximum picture benefits. Home video frequently "looks" like home video because of inadequate lighting. All video cameras work best when their apertures are set to at least $f/4$. Smaller apertures are better than wider apertures. Even those cameras with controls for optimizing light sensitivity cannot provide their best pictures under "worst" lighting conditions.

What would seem to be the easiest way to achieve increased lighting is to place higher-wattage bulbs in the lamps and fixtures of the room in which you're shooting. But this rarely provides enough lighting to overcome the low-light problem. Usually a movie light at the least, for short-duration scenes, will help considerably. Better still is the use of video lights. These relatively inexpensive yet ominous-looking units can provide enough light to create videophotography that rivals broadcast quality on the home screen. Two 600-watt quartz lamps will provide enough lighting in the average living room or bedroom to quickly justify their expense because of improved picture quality. A third quartz lamp may also be desired for highlighting specific areas of your subject matter.

The standard professional lighting approach is to use two main lights for the room, possibly shining them directly onto the subject at 45-degree angles or bouncing them off the ceiling. A third spotlight is suggested for highlighting a subject or eliminating shadows behind the subject. While many books have been written on the subject of lighting in photography, for our purposes experi-

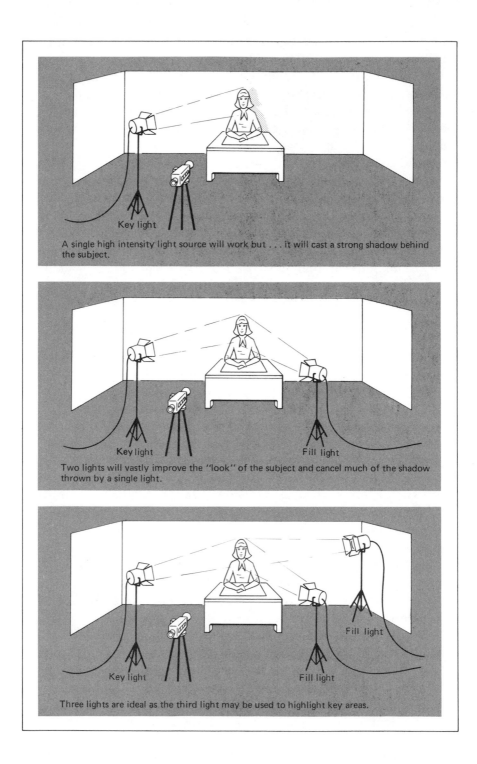

A single high intensity light source will work but . . . it will cast a strong shadow behind the subject.

Two lights will vastly improve the "look" of the subject and cancel much of the shadow thrown by a single light.

Three lights are ideal as the third light may be used to highlight key areas.

mentation is certainly the best teacher. Remember, the idea is to provide enough light for the camera to produce its best picture, and to make the light look as natural as possible at the same time. A three-light quartz arrangement should provide enough light for virtually any home video situation. Two lights are the minimum recommended under any circumstances.

> *Note*: While all home video cameras can produce pictures under almost any low-light condition, the price of low light is seen as a loss of picture detail, color quality, and an increase in video noise—static. In addition, as light falls off, in order to compensate, the camera will automatically open its lens. The more the lens opens, the less of the subject area it can focus on at one time. At $f/8$ or $f/11$ subjects from a few feet (.3 m) to many feet away will be in focus. At $f/1.8$ or $f/1.4$, subjects will be in focus over a range of only a foot or two to a range of several inches (2 cm). This is called a loss of depth of field and is true of all photography, film or video.

Again, and we cannot stress it enough, make a rule to provide as much light on your subject as you can, under any circumstances. By keeping the aperture of the video camera at its mid-range setting, maximum picture values will be derived and focusing requirements will be reduced. Rest assured, the results will always be worth the extra effort. And if your sunlit videophotography has frequently looked better than your indoor work, you probably now know why.

Set Design in video photography is simple and sensible in nature. Few home video photographers have the room or the finances to set up a studio for their work. In the absence of a studio, there are some rules that apply to all cinematography.

The set should not intrude upon the subject being photographed. It should be the setting, the background, but never the subject itself.

In color TV work you will note an absence of overly bright background colors. This is because they are both distracting to the viewer and may cause a color shift to take place that makes it impossible to correctly balance the background color to the flesh tones of the subject. So, please don't use bright red rooms for camera work.

STEPS IN SETTING UP A VIDEO CAMERA

ATTACH CAMERA TO SUPPORT

If a tripod or other such support is to be used, first attach the camera to the support using the screw mount on the camera's base. This may be located on the camera body proper or on the bottom of the hand grip.

PLUG IN CABLES

Whether or not a support is to be used, the camera's connecting cables must be plugged into their proper receptables on the VCR, the CCU (camera control unit) or the AC adapter. Some cameras require a CCU and these units come with the camera when you buy it. Some camera/VCR combinations require a separate AC adapter. In either case the cables must be properly connected, before the equipment can be operated. The cables are polarized and shaped to prevent a wrong connection.

TURN ON VCR

Turn on the VCR to energize the cables leading to the video-camera. If an AC adapter is being used plug that into 110 VAC power and turn on the adapter.

TURN ON CAMERA

Remember it is preferred to turn the camera on and off with its own power switch rather than leaving it on and controlling it from the VCR.

ADJUST COLOR TEMPERATURE AND WHITE BALANCE

Once the camera is on wait a moment or two for it to warm-up. First set the camera's color temperature and white balance. Since each camera is different, some will have one or two controls for this purpose and scalar charts on the side. Some will have a single button for the purpose and set themselves automatically. Follow the manufacturers instructions for setting color temperature and white balance.

USE TV AS MONITOR
If you are shooting indoors, you may want to make use of a color TV as a monitor. In that case plug the VCR's VHF output into the TV monitor. Adjust the TV set for proper color rendition (tune in a broadcast channel to make this adjustment) and switch the TV to the VCR's output channel. Then set the color controls of the camera for the most accurate color balance.

FRAME AND FOCUS
The next step is framing the subject and focusing. Look through the viewfinder of the camera or if you are using a monitor use that instead. Then simply zoom in on the subject area and focus the lens. Once focused, zoom out to frame the subject area to your preference.

SET UP SEPARATE MICS
If separate mics are to be used they, too, must be set properly. This means placing them as close as possible to the subject. They must be plugged into the camera's Mic Input, or if the camera has no Mic Input, into the VCR's Mic Input. Always test the performance of a microphone before using it for the first time. Also if the mic is powered by a battery, be sure it is working properly.

SET VCR TO RECORD AND SHOOT
Note: The exact sequence for your particular VCR/video-camera combination may vary somewhat from that just outlined. There are really no hard-and-fast rules to setting-up a videocamera, and trial and error is the best way to learn. Keep in mind that powering should be controlled by the on/off switch of the camera, the CCU, or AC adapter. You probably won't do any harm if you control the camera power from the VCR. (But why take a chance?) Also, things can go wrong during a shoot, so check and double-check as often as possible, especially if you are shooting a once-in-a-lifetime event.

Also, where possible, use as simple a background as possible for your work. The old rule about not placing your subject in front of a tree in such a way that the tree seems to be growing out of the subject's head applies in video. Distracting backgrounds simply detract from the subject and should be avoided.

Many of the companies serving the semiprofessional and professional markets sell floor standing screens for the purpose of providing suitable backgrounds. These screens are printed to look like various familiar settings. We have all seen people on broadcast television being interviewed in their libraries. The fact is that frequently these libraries only exist on the front panels of a screen carried in the van of the TV crew. Other such backgrounds are available. If you plan on interviewing a number of people, often, the fairly high investment in such a screen may be warranted.

Otherwise, keep the background simple, be sure that there is enough room for the equipment you will need and that the area to be photographed is well lit.

GRAPHICS

Graphics are simply written words, charts, illustrations, etc. Titles and credits are an example of graphics used universally on all broadcast video programs.

The degree to which you can and wish to use graphics will determine your interest in them. Used properly, they can make a home video presentation look a great deal more professional. Their absence, however, will not be readily noticed, as most people are not used to seeing graphics during home video or movie shows.

Fortunately, most home video camera lenses feature a "macro" setting, with lenses capable of being focused on objects only a few inches away. If your camera does not have a macro setting, some of the graphics available cannot be used by you. However, others can be used so don't spend a lot of time fretting about it.

Advanced amateurs, with large pocketbooks, may choose to work with more than one camera, using one for the subject, the other for a graphic. We will limit ourselves to the single camera home video hobbiest.

Shooting signs on buildings, billboards, or on lampposts, etc. can provide a frame of reference if you begin an on-location presentation with such footage. Closeups of books, photographs, whatever, with your own lettering positioned on top will also give your presentation a professional look, especially if you begin by fading onto the lettering (image starts out dark and becomes light).

To do this simply, place the title on a suitable background, set all camera controls and manually close down the aperture control to its minimum setting, $f/16$ or $f/22$. Start the VCR and open the lens to provide proper exposure. This fade-in on lettering can be quite an attention getter. So, too, can be shooting titles through glass and then zooming through the titles to the subject behind them.

With the same kind of prepared letter sets used for home moviemaking, some colored cardboard stock, you're set to go. Or an especially effective trick is to affix the letters to clear glass and shoot the titles through the glass. This gives an effect similar to the two-camera professional approach. Just be sure the glass is held steady and that the camera's aperture is stopped down enough to keep both the graphics and the scene behind them in focus.

As for lighting, experimentation is the key to exciting visual effects with graphics. Let your imagination run wild—what you don't like can always be erased.

SCRIPTING

Another area of production often ignored by home video enthusiasts is scripting. The most professional, smoothest-looking productions have, at the least, a basic flow to them. We are not suggesting that home video be used for professional-looking productions all of the time. That would take much of the fun and spontaneity out of it. What we are suggesting is that you have an idea of how you would like your scenes to flow. You should tell the people who will be in front of the camera what they are to do, in advance of shooting. You may prepare them for your video camerawork by giving them sufficient background information about how long the scene will last, where they should stand or sit, where you will be shooting from, how loudly to speak into the microphone, etc. All of these aspects of home video are part of scripting. You may, of course, elect to write a script for your performers. But, in most cases, a short talk before the scene is shot should do the trick. The idea is that everyone have a good idea of what is expected and of what to expect. This will make everybody's life easier and prevent frayed nerves and tempers. If you are shooting at home, it's a good idea to leave the phone off the hook. Whether you call this scripting or directing is an academic decision. Just see to it that it is done and your shooting should go well.

WORKING WITH PEOPLE
Most people, certainly friends and relatives, are willing to be helpful in the production of home video. It's still a new experience to them and, like the first instant photography, home video invites active participation on the part of strangers.

Other than ensuring you have their permission to tape them, or in the case of a professional, you have a signed model release, the basic rules of scripting and directing are all you need apply. Remember, the fewer on-camera surprises, the better.

If you are shooting in the field, all sorts of people will appear in front of your lens, usually at the most inopportune times. If it serves your purpose to include them, by all means do so, and remember, like instant photography, an electronic viewfinder affords you the option of playing back what you have just photographed.

With professional talent, you will have to tell them what is expected. Professional performers are used to being directed. Do not expect, or demand, that they simply perform for you, even if you are paying them a fee. See to it that they know what is expected, how long the performance is to be, from what angles they will be shot, and so on.

SETTING UP THE SHOT
By this time, we hope you will be more aware of the need to plan, even minimally, your shots. In setting up a shot there are certain basic considerations to keep in mind. There must be sufficient lighting, sufficient room for all the people who will be in front of the camera, sufficient room for you to work. At the least, you must know the wide-angle capability of your camera, for not every camera can handle every kind of indoor shot you will want to try.

Video is a medium of closeups. Your camera will always provide capacity for these kinds of shots but may not give you the wide-angle capability you will need. Frequently videographers find themselves standing up against a wall in a room, or have to learn to live with panning, because they cannot include everyone they want on-screen at the same time. This is where planning really pays off. Try to select indoor settings large enough to accom-

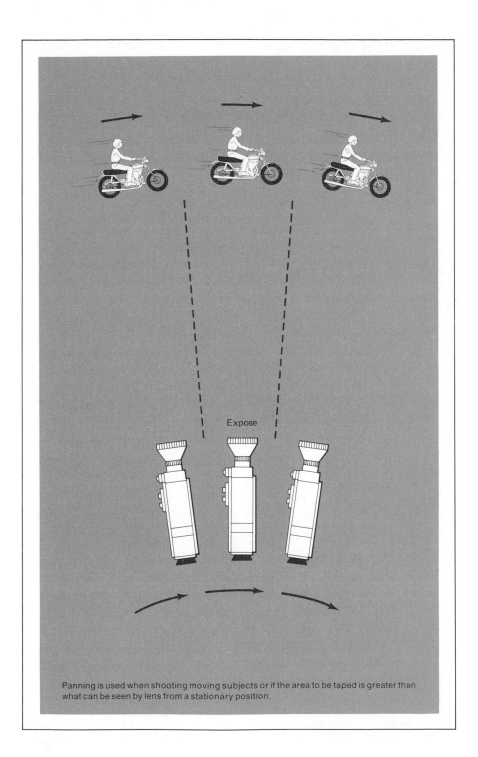

Expose

Panning is used when shooting moving subjects or if the area to be taped is greater than what can be seen by lens from a stationary position.

modate all the people you want to include in the shot. Make sure the room or area is well lit. Ensure that everyone does not talk at once, or that they are individually miked. Plan your shots to flatter the people being videotaped. Some people look better head on, some in profile, others with a slightly diffused look.

If you have the time, try to practice the shot with nobody in the scene. See how it looks through the camera. This same rule applies outdoors. If you have time before a shot, check the framing through the camera. Sometimes just a few feet of difference in the camera position will have a powerful effect on the look of the shot.

In sum, the more your subjects know about what is expected, the more you think about how to frame your shots, the better lit the scene, the less intrusive the background is, the more professional your final production will be.

EDITING IN THE CAMERA

In video, it is essential that most or all of your editing be done in the camera—at the time you shoot it. The reason is simple. Most people do not own or contemplate buying a second VCR. What's more, half-inch video was never really intended to be edited. The best way to edit home formats is to rerecord the segments wanted, in the order they are wanted, onto three-quarter-inch videotape. When the final production is completed, it is rerecorded back down to the half-inch home format. This method is terribly expensive, as it necessitates renting time in a professional studio (costs range from $25 to $100 per hour).

So the best rule is to plan to edit in the camera. This requires a reasonable amount of planning before each shot is placed onto the tape. It requires that the *PAUSE* control of the camera be used whenever possible, rather than the *STOP* control. But pausing may only be accomplished for short periods of time, as previously explained. The *PAUSE* control provides a cleaner, almost invisible, in-camera edit. Going into *STOP* may create short spans of noise on the tape—called, in video parlance, "glitches."

In video, as opposed to movies, it is essential to plan the sequence of shots before shooting them, not to shoot and think about resequencing them later. Film is easy to edit at home—tape is not.

If you must edit tape, you will need two VCRs (assuming that you do not wish to utilize a professional videotape production house because it is simply too costly). One of the VCRs will contain the original footage to be edited, the other will contain blank tape on which the selected scene will be rerecorded. From that point on, editing is accomplished simply by rerecording the original footage in the order preferred.

EXPERIMENTING WITH EFFECTS

The most often used special effect in video is zooming in and away from a subject. Fade-ins and fade-outs follow in popularity. A third special effect is the phenomenon of feedback. From any audio work you may have done, you probably know that if you are using a microphone and hold it too close to a loudspeaker it will howl horribly. This is called "feedback." In video, feedback may be used for creating all manner of visual distortions such as multiple images or pulsating light patterns.

To create video feedback, sit in front of a TV screen on which you can monitor your VCR's output. Connect your video camera to the VCR and tape from and monitor the TV screen at the same time. You may do this without actually taping, if you wish, by setting the VCR as though taping, but placing it in the *PAUSE* mode. The idea is to get the camera to see its own image through the TV screen and cause a feedback condition.

The effect can be staggering. By playing with the camera—its angle towards the TV screen, its aperture opening, and its focus—all manner of strange images can be created. When you find one you like, record it.

Most of the special-effects attachments (filters) that can be used on movie camera lenses can also be used on video camera lenses. Possibilities include star-burst effects, soft-focus effects, color enhancement, and many more. For more information on filters and special effects that they can create see *The Complete Tiffen Filter Manual* (Amphoto; 1981).

We suggest that when you get to the point of wishing to enhance your productions with special effects, simply pay a visit to your local camera supply shop. Remember to bring your video camera so that you will purchase the correct size filter, and if you wish, also bring the VCR and experiment in the store.

Remember that titling may be considered a special effect, as can fading in and out, zooming in and out, and that by combining these with video feedback you can almost equal the best of Hollywood.

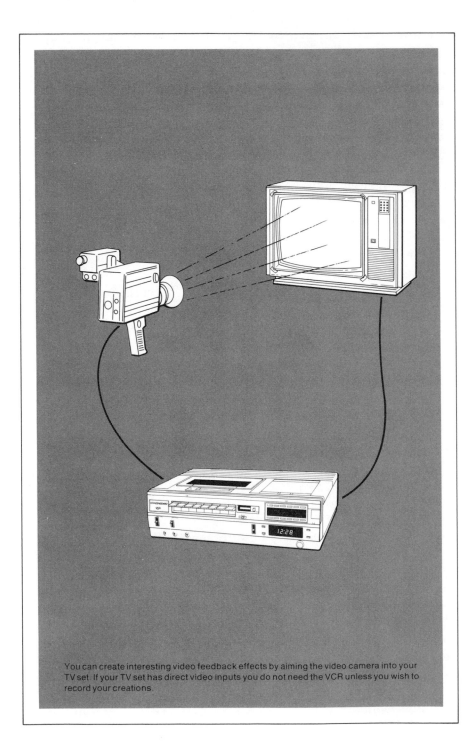

You can create interesting video feedback effects by aiming the video camera into your TV set. If your TV set has direct video inputs you do not need the VCR unless you wish to record your creations.

USING TWO CAMERAS

In professional work, switching between and among cameras plays a major role in making these productions look "professional." It is probably the most obvious difference between home cinematography and broadcast. Yet to get the two camera-look may be as easy as shooting one person at a time, pausing, and changing camera position for the other person. This can be carried out to include outdoor subjects as well. Change camera position often, try to simulate the two-camera approach, and see how well it works.

The difficulty in using two cameras for a home video production lies not in the double cost, although that is reason enough for most of us, but in an electronic fact of life. Simply put, home cameras are not made to synchronize with one another.

If you are wondering what synchronization has to do with video, think of what happens when you change TV channels at home. Frequently the picture rolls for a moment or two. That is because the television set has to get in sync with the image being broadcast. Once it does, all is well.

With video cameras the same thing holds true, particularly for the VCR. If you take two or three cameras, plug them into the video equivalent of an audio mixing device, and feed the output to a VCR, every time you switch to another camera the picture may roll. This happens because the picture signals are not in sync. You would get not the professional look, but an appearance of faulty equipment.

The only exception to the rule is that some manufacturers have made what are called "special effects generators" (SEGs) to work within their own home systems. One of these systems has a SEG that contains its own black-and-white camera. This camera is meant for adding titles. The SEG contains the circuits necessary to maintain synchronization (prevents picture roll) with the primary camera, which is the color camera actually used for shooting your subjects. The advantage of this one system is that it allows you to place color titles on any portion of the production you wish, as long as you have sufficient manpower to operate all the equipment and the money to pay for it.

With this single exception, multiple-camera work has not been brought to the home video level. The only way to achieve it is to use and buy industrial equipment, which, while not that much more expensive, is a bit more difficult to handle.

Shown are two VCRs hooked up for postproduction editing.

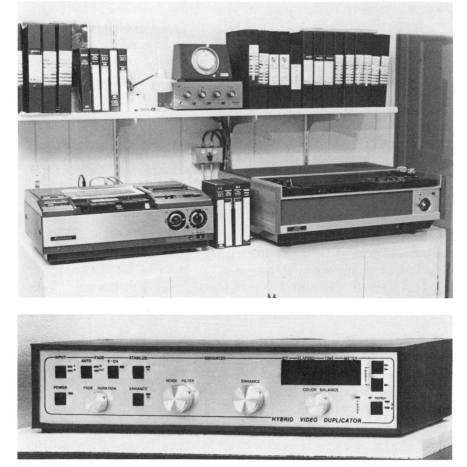

This deluxe video duplicator is equipped with many features to enhance and professionalize the look of your postproduction work.

POSTPRODUCTION
TECHNIQUES

After you have completed all the steps of recording home video, there are two things you can do. Either show the footage exactly as shot, unedited, or take it through the various stages of editing and enhancement referred to as "postproduction."

Most often you will probably elect the former and show the production verbatim. There is nothing wrong in doing so. It's quicker, involves less work, and is just plain fun. However, there may be times when you will want to give your productions a more polished look, or when they will not suffice as they were shot because of overly long or out-of-sequence scenes, poor audio, lack of special effects or titles, etc.

Having an idea of just what you can do is essential. From that point on, it's entirely up to you. In fact, moans and yawns from an audience can provide more inspiration than all the words we could ever write on the subject.

AUDIO DUBBING

Audio dubbing is something of a misnomer. In reality we mean replacing the original audio with a new soundtrack. To accomplish this you will need to prepare a soundtrack in advance or use music and other sounds, live or recorded, to rerecord over the original.

Dubbing is most useful if you must replace an entire soundtrack. It will not pay to try and replace specific portions of an otherwise useful soundtrack, as audio continuity may be lost and the discontinuity becomes obvious.

The easiest way to add a new soundtrack is through a microphone connected to your VCR. As you play back the tape, simply press the dubbing button on the VCR and play the new soundtrack or speak into the microphone. The new sound will be recorded over the old soundtrack. If you wish to mix the old soundtrack with the new, you will have to use an audio recorder and record the old soundtrack onto it. You may then play the original soundtrack through the audio recorder and add new sounds to it using the microphone input and dubbing control of the VCR.

Of course, the same effect may be created, with better audio fidelity, by direct wiring, if you create a whole new soundtrack on audio tape first and then play it back directly into the VCR.

The only problem with dubbing is that if any of the original material is to be kept, lip-synchronization will probably be lost. There is nothing you can do about this. Professional equipment can prevent the problem, but no home video gear can.

Each VCR is somewhat different in how it effects the dubbing procedure. All will accommodate a microphone or line (wire) input. Please refer to your owner's manual for exact details.

VIDEOTAPE DUBBING AND EDITING
Making duplicate tapes can be as simple as connecting a single wire between two VCRs; or no more complex than connecting two cables between two VCRs.

On all VCRs there are line inputs and outputs. They are usually called *VIDEO IN / VIDEO OUT* and *AUDIO IN / AUDIO OUT*. For the best possible quality in dubbing, these direct input and output connectors should be used. To use them you will need cables fitted with the proper plugs to mate with your equipment's terminals. Because these terminals differ from machine to machine, please check your owner's manual for the proper type of connectors to purchase.

A simpler connection can be made from the VHF output of recorder A to the VHF input of recorder B. The only problem is that some video quality (detail, color, sharpness) will be lost in the transfer, and in home video you cannot afford to lose quality. It is therefore preferable to use line inputs and output for dubbing from tape to tape.

The other requirements, of course, are two VCRs. Contrary to myth, any format VCR can be used with any other format VCR for making copies of tape. Obviously, format A tapes dubbed on format B machines will only play on format B machines. But the transfer can be made either way. Similarly, if a tape is to be edited, it can be edited on any VCR from quarter-inch to broadcast size.

When editing or dubbing from machine to machine, try and use the better of the two machines to record the final copy of the material. In other words, use the poorer machine to play the original tape into the better machine, on which you will make the final recording. Also, use the best quality tape you can buy for the VCR that will record the final tape. High-grade tapes can be a little less noisy than regular-grade tape, and noise is the big problem of video dubbing.

Whether you choose the simpler RF route (*VHF OUT* to *VHF IN*) or the somewhat more troublesome, but higher quality, line route (*VIDEO/AUDIO OUT* to *VIDEO/AUDIO IN*), there will be some noticeable quality loss in the transfer process.

This is a reality of home video. The system was not devised to provide excellent dubbing capabilities, but to provide excellent original taping and playback capabilities. This is why we repeat the importance of editing in the camera whenever possible.

The original tape you shot is referred to as first-generation tape, the copy as second-generation tape, and so on. Only broadcast-quality equipment can make perfect second-generation or third-generation copies.

To aid in the dubbing process, many video enhancement accessories are marketed and we will discuss those, and their effects on video, shortly.

The process of "assemble editing" is the dubbing of an original tape onto a second tape with scenes in their proper order. This is about the most you can do in terms of postproduction editing. And as mentioned, there will be some loss of quality in the process.

As with tape copying, or straight dubbing, two VCRs are necessary. Again, line-to-line inputting is preferred, but you can go RF and use the *VHF OUT* to feed the *VHF IN* of the second machine.

To assemble edit, place your original tape in machine A and a blank videocassette in machine B. Machine A should be set to *PLAYBACK*, machine B to *RECORD*.

For the most troublefree edits, use the *PAUSE* control of machine B rather than the *STOP* control when it is necessary to halt the editing process.

To edit, simply play back on machine A the material you want to record. Start the tape a little before the actual material appears, to allow the machine to get up to running speed. Similarly, place machine B in the *RECORD* mode and immediately place machine B in *PAUSE*. When the correct material appears on machine A, which you can tell by monitoring it on your TV set, release the *PAUSE* control on machine B. Machine B will now record the signal from machine A until machine B is placed in *PAUSE* once again. This should be exactly where you want the scene you are editing to end. With machine B in *PAUSE*, locate the second scene on machine A and rewind machine A slightly. Then play back scene two on machine A and when you get to the start of the second scene release the *PAUSE* control of machine B. Carry out this process until everything is recorded the way you want it on machine B. This is called assemble editing because you have assembled the scenes in the sequence you want on the second tape in machine B. Now you may decide to provide the edited program with a new soundtrack, or leave the old soundtrack intact.

Once you are familiar with this procedure, it is easy to add new scenes to the original material or perhaps place a credit line using graphics at the beginning or end of your production. If you are going to require additional editing, do not erase your original tape. The quality of a dub from the edited tape will be so poor, you will wish you had never started to edit in the first place.

If your footage is valuable enough, you may wish to edit using the facilities of a production house. These companies will be found in your Yellow Pages. They are costly to use, but you will not lose quality (and in fact with image enhancement may even gain a little in the process). For truly important tape editing using a production house is the only sensible thing to do.

FILM-TO-TAPE TRANSFERS

It is easy to transfer your photographs to videotape with a camera. Movies on the other hand, pose a problem for home video transfer. For most people the best way to transfer films to tape is to have it done professionally.

Telecine converters are devices sold to make this transfer easy and possible. The trouble is, they don't work very well. It's easy to see why.

Film is shot at 18 or 24 frames per second. That means that each second, either 18 or 24 still pictures are taken by a movie camera. Video, however, shoots its pictures at the rate of 30 frames per second. (Believe us, this is true, even though you can't see the frames on videotape.)

Obviously the different frame rates do not jibe, and some adjustment should be made. If not, the transferred film may flicker when it is placed on videotape.

The professional transfer houses and services have equipment designed specifically for making these frame rate adjustments. The home telecine converter does not. Sometimes it will work just fine, if you're lucky, and sometimes it will produce an unviewable result.

The converter itself is a simple device. Into one end, you project, using a projector, your movies or slides. They show onto a small, built-in screen, upon which you focus your video camera. That's about all there is to it. If all goes well you can convert a movie or videotape your home movies with satisfactory results.

Additionally, if you wish, you can use the color temperature adjustments on the video camera to adjust for off-colors in your original movies, or to enhance their colors if the film has faded. If you have an extension speaker for the projector you can also enhance the sound by placing the video microphone a distance away from the racket of the projector. If your projector has an audio output you could transfer the sound by direct wire. If it only has a speaker output a cable may be connected across the speaker terminals, or a local service store can modify your projector to enable a direct audio transfer.

Sound may be added later. Appropriate music with a running commentary is often the most appreciated accompaniment to a slide show. But no matter, worry about the sound after you've made the conversion.

SLIDE-TO-TAPE TRANSFERS

Transferring 35mm slides to videotape can considerably enhance your slide collection. Using the same telecine device designed for transferring super 8 film to videotape, set up your video camera and projector according to the instructions supplied with the telecine adapter. *Or you may project onto a movie screen.*

Be sure to remember to align the slide projector parallel to the telecine's small screen. The video camera must also be parallel to the reflective surface that will display the projected image that is to be recorded. To check the image put the VCR into *RECORD* and use your TV as a monitor to position the picture on the screen.

It is preferable to use a telephoto lens so you can zoom into the projected image and focus as sharply as possible. Frame the image

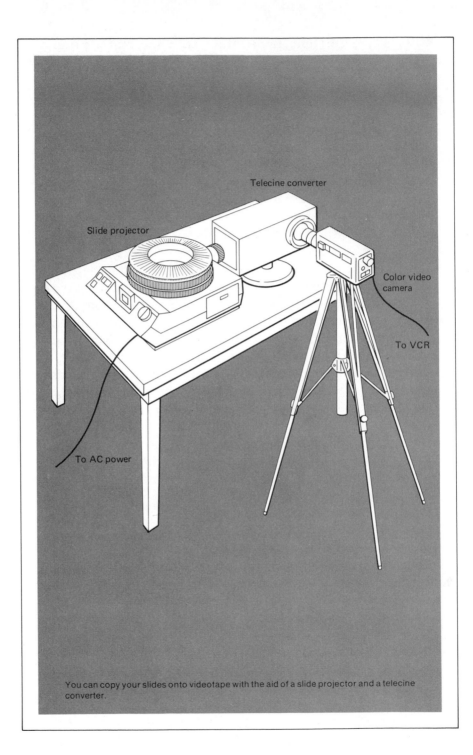

Slide projector

Telecine converter

Color video camera

To VCR

To AC power

You can copy your slides onto videotape with the aid of a slide projector and a telecine converter.

Because the shape of a TV screen and a 35mm slide are quite different it is often necessary to crop your slides down to the most important element in the picture.

either by zooming in close enough to emphasize only a portion of the image or you may want to show the entire image leaving blank space at the top and bottom (this is unavoidable because the proportions of a slide differ from those of a TV screen).

At this point you are ready to begin recording. Dim the room lights to increase the image's brightness. To enhance your slide show you may want to add motion by moving the camera and create effects by adjusting the camera controls.

An audio track may be recorded simultaneously as you move through the slide sequence or it can be dubbed in after the video recording is completed. You may want to use music from a tape player, a record, or live sound using a mic.

USING ACCESSORIES
TO ENHANCE YOUR PRODUCTION

The number of video accessories on the market is staggering. However, only a few are used for postproduction. Video stabilizers and enhancers are two types of basic devices that you can use to enhance your video tapes.

The stabilizer is used in making copies of prerecorded tape (which, by the way, is illegal) and to aid older television sets in handling these tapes which usually include an antitheft signal (shows as a weakened sync signal).

Older televisions tend to have a picture roll problem and so may require stabilizers. That is how stabilizers got onto the market in the first place. Also, some of the older VCRs may not be able to handle signals coded against copying. The stabilizer overcomes the antitheft coding and restores normal playback to these prerecorded tapes.

The image enhancers that are made for the home video enthusiast may actually make editing easier and the edited tape better. They only work on video signals, however, and are used in-line and not at the RF stages. In other words, they cannot be used between the VHF output of recorder A and the VHF input of recorder B. They can be used in-between the *VIDEO OUT* of recorder A and the *VIDEO IN* of recorder B. They can help reduce signal noise, sharpen picture detail, and maintain a strong color level in the signal. If you are going to do a lot of editing, a video enhancer may be a very valuable friend. Ask to try one first before you buy it—a good general rule to follow with all video equipment. Some of these enhancers contain controls that allow you to fade to black. This means that as you edit you can fade out one scene and fade into another—a neat trick. Of course you can also do so with the camera, but if you forgot, it's an added plus if the enhancer you are contemplating has a fader built-in. Some enhancers also contain video amplifiers, enabling you to make several enhanced copies at once.

TIPS ON REPAIRING VIDEOCASSETTES

No matter how careful you are, no matter the brand, sooner or later a tape is going to break in a cassette. When this happens what do you do? While some books and articles in hobby magazines tell you how to open the cassette and splice the broken tape, it still seems most prudent not to do it yourself. If the job is done wrong, you will lose not only the tape, but also the use of your machine as well (while it is out in the repair shop getting new tape heads installed).

The best method is to take the broken tape to a production house and let them transfer it to a brand-new cassette. At best, a splice would only allow you to do the same thing at home. Nobody, but nobody, recommends splicing videotape and using it as though it were undamaged.

If only the leader has separated from the hub, inside the cassette, you may have a chance to save the cassette without having to rerecord it. But you still should seek a professional to make the repair.

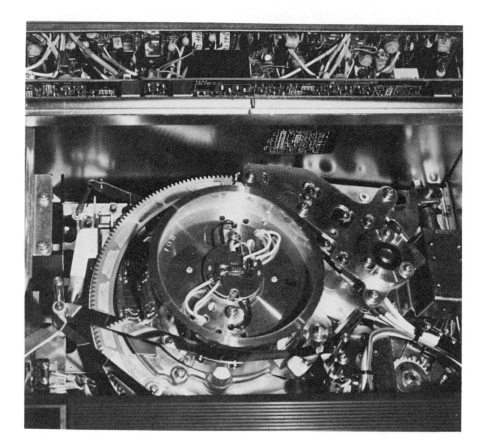

5

EQUIPMENT MAINTENANCE

The videocassette recorder is your personal vehicle for escape from the programming and time constrictions of commercial broadcast television. Just like any prized vehicle it must be kept in tiptop shape to perform properly.

A good general rule concerning the VCR and videocassettes is that moisture and dust or other minute foreign particles are to be avoided at all costs. If you are not careful they will cause nothing but damage to your equipment and, ultimately, to the picture you see on the TV screen.

When your recorder is idle, keep the dustcover or lid on to minimize the settling of normal room dust on sensitive parts. Whether your model is a tabletop or a portable type, select a place for it in your home where no direct sunlight can reach it and where temperature and humidity average 70F (21C) and 50 percent, respectively.

Constantly keeping the VCR's heads, head drum, and tape guides clean and free from external substances is your best guarantee of troublefree operation and picture playback quality.

HEADS

The only part of the machine that should be cleaned by inexperienced hobbyists is the tape heads. You won't have to go inside the machine in order to periodically clean the heads. There are many head-cleaning cassettes available that are designed to slip into the VCR just like a regular cassette. Putting the machine into *PLAY* (with a head-cleaning cassette in place) for a few seconds (refer to the instructions included with individual cassette brands) will remove unwanted tape residue and other matter from tape heads.

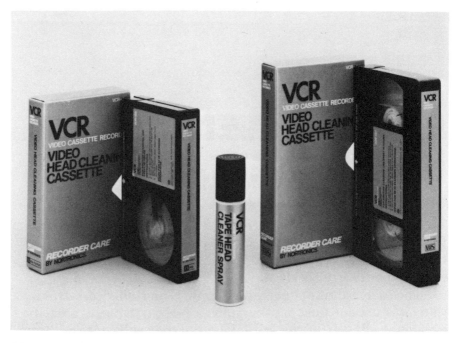

You should clean the heads of your VCR after every fifty, or so, hours of use. The easiest way to do so is to use a head-cleaning cassette like the ones shown here.

When using head-cleaning cassettes, however, be very careful not to overuse them, as this may result in severe damage to the heads. If the heads are damaged beyond repair replacement can be an expensive proposition depending on where you have your machine serviced.

If you're handy and have experience with other similar mechanical or electronics repair, you can graduate to the procedure that entails removing the machine's upper casing and making direct contact with the heads, head drum, and tape guides for more extensive cleaning.

Cleaning the heads after every fifty hours of use and having the VCR checked by a professional service shop once a year (for heavy users) or once every two years (for less regular users) should suffice in most cases.

Others have advised that VCR heads should be replaced after every one-thousand hours of use, yet we have never seen a VCR with that many hours (or even more hours) that suffered from worn tape heads. The VCR is generally a more rugged and reliable instrument than some manufacturers give it credit for being. Most will easily outlast the conservative estimates of how long certain of its parts may be operated before replacement is warranted.

As a rule, for nonportables, keep the unit rock-steady and give it periodic check ups especially if you notice the picture begin to deteriorate. If severe problems develop, haul it into the shop. Don't tamper with it yourself. In this case, when possible, try to use the manufacturer's own service department or a well staffed authorized service center.

VCR

Paralleling the maintenance of a fuel-driven vehicle—the car—the VCR needs to be lubricated and have its belts (when applicable) replaced every now and again.

In the case of portables, recharge the battery after every use or at least every six months, when idle, and keep the VCR in its carrying case when recording away from home.

Extra care should be taken when toting your video recording equipment to the beach, where salt in the air and water can pose a double dose of danger to your machine. Likewise, recording in extremely cold weather (32F [35C] or less) calls for added protection measures. A favorite technique is wrapping the VCR and camera, separately, in plastic bags or a similar housing. Nature's elements are not kind to the VCR and camera, so if you want to brave the elements, you'll have to dress your equipment to stay warm and dry as carefully as you would dress yourself.

CAMERA

The camera has fewer moving parts than the VCR so there is a lot less to keep clean inside it, but there are still parts of the unit that must be cared for.

When not using the video camera, always keep the lens cap on, and use the iris (aperture) control to "close down" the lens. That is, always set it to the highest f number on the lens—$f/16$ or $f/22$. Remember, the camera is light-sensitive, so it is critical to constantly control the amount of light entering the lens even when the camera is off. Too much light will permanently damage the photosensitive Vidicon tube within the camera, possibly leaving a lasting "burn-in" spot, which will be visible on your TV screen if you use the camera after the damage has occurred.

Never allow the camera lens to be pointed directly toward the sun or other high-intensity light source. This will cause irreparable damage to the tube in the worst way possible. Also store the camera with the lens slanted slightly upward so that any internal debris will not adhere to the inner face of the Vidicon tube.

The lens needs special consideration. Wiping it with a soft, dry cloth or brush is a good, quick way to keep it dirt-free. When changing lenses, do not allow any dust to enter the inside of the camera, where it can harm the tube, or point the camera body at a direct source of light.

Don't leave the camera anywhere you wouldn't leave your VCR, as it is subject to suffering from the same adverse conditions as is the VCR.

TAPE

Taking care of blank tape would seem to be a simple matter, but there's a lot to remember if you want to effectively protect and prolong the life of your tape.

A quality videocassette should be safe to use for one-hundred to two-hundred passes. (Each time the tape is run through a VCR, whether in *RECORD* or *PLAY*, it's called a "pass.")

The magnetic coating on a low-grade or overused cassette will eventually flake off, and some will remain on the heads of the VCR. Dirty heads cannot record or play back a clean image. This same process occurs more slowly and gradually with any tape, which is why it's advisable to regularly clean the machine's heads.

Store the tapes on a flat surface, arranging them like books, vertically, so the length of the spine is facing outward. Always keep cassettes in their sleeves. For added protection, keep tapes in a sealed plastic case.

Don't expose the tape itself to any dust, moisture, humidity, or direct sunlight. Another foe of cassettes is any kind of magnetic field created by electrical items and motors, which can disturb any information that may be recorded on a tape. Do not place tapes on or near speakers or electronic gear.

Cassettes go through a long and winding path after they've been inserted into the VCR. It's not a good idea to leave a cassette in the still-frame mode for too long a time, and always remove the cas-

sette from the machine after you've finished using it.

Don't overuse the *PAUSE* mode when using your deck; rather try to make efficient use of the *STOP* control—it will rescue the tape from some unnecessary stress.

Brand-new tapes fresh out of their wrapping are sometimes wound so tightly that it can help if you run the tape through the machine in fast forward and then rewind before recording. Tape has a tendency to buckle, so take every opportunity to give it a chance to relax. Tape that doesn't run smoothly through the maze of the tape path will not record nor will it play back properly.

Don't every force open the cassette's hinged lid. Placing one hand at either end of the lid, you can gently use your fingers to open the lid after releasing its safety catch.

A recorded videocassette that you want to prevent from accidental erasure can be made erase-proof. Notice a tab at the end of the front spine on the cassette. It's cut out on three sides. Breaking off this small plastic square will make recording impossible. To reuse the cassette, you can place a piece of tape over the broken off square to restore recording capability.

After a tape has completed its playback or record cycle, don't rewind it, but leave it that way. Rewind it before the next use. This procedure evaporates any residual moisture that may have formed while the cassette was sitting idle.

As a matter of convenience versus care, it's smart to devise a sensible system for cataloging your cassettes early on. The method you choose is immaterial as long as it's easy to follow and efficient. You might prefer your library of video programs to be sorted according to chronological order of the recording, subject matter, or genre.

Having an organized collection will help you to make maximum use of each minute on a cassette and will save you time and aggravation when searching for a tape to play or to record on.

6

THE MANY USES OF HOME VIDEO

NEWS EVENTS

How many times have you relived history by looking back through old yellowed newspapers and clippings to recall a memorable event? Each time, the experience sends a tingle through your body. Imagine, then, having at your disposal a video version of history as recorded through the eyes of the media.

Noteworthy events that are both planned (the Royal Wedding of Prince Charles and Lady Diana) and of the moment (the dramatic release of the American hostages in Iran in January 1981, on the same day as President Ronald Reagan's inauguration) can be recorded by stationing yourself at the controls of your VCR and holding vigil during the course of an unfolding news event, pausing for commercials if you desire, or editing as you go. A second VCR for dubbing and editing "raw" tapes will help give all your off-air archival tapes a finished, better-paced look.

Following the directions from chapter 4 on postproduction, select the highlights of the tape, change their sequence perhaps, and record only those on the second "editing" VCR. There may be portions of the visual program where the broadcast audio can be deleted. In those spots you can add your own music or other audio track.

Visual records of moving national and international news events become a dramatic and effective means of traveling back in time, but there's another, more significant application. The tapes can be used as educational aids for your children, affording them access to "You Are There" presentations of history in the making.

A similar anthology can be collected by the eagle-eyed video recordist, comprised of outstanding performances on TV variety programs, full-length works presented on public broadcasting stations, championship sporting events, and many more possible program categories.

CREATING A FAMILY ALBUM

A home video recording system is the ideal medium for chronicling your family history. You can watch the production proceedings on the TV to keep restless tykes occupied while you are setting up shots. The tapes can be played back instantly, giving you the luxury of restaging the entire scene if you're dissatisfied with the results you got.

You don't need to haul out an unwieldy projector, set up a screen, and dim the lights before settling back to view the movie to the noisy accompaniment of whirring reels of film. On videotape, just slip the cassette into the VCR attached to your TV, press *PLAY*, and you're ready to watch your "Family Frolics" tape.

The first tapes you may want to make for your video family album are shots of your family's photograph album. Use the macro setting on a zoom lens, mount the camera on a camera stand (found in any photo supply store) or tripod and throw abundant light on the subject. You can lend a nice human touch to the production by slowly turning the pages of the album, using your finger as a pointer. The soundtrack can include a narrative in your own voice, reminiscing as you free-associate with the photos. Playing softly under your voice, in the background, use an appropriate musical selection.

If you prefer a more businesslike approach, you can speed up the pace of the programs, eliminate the hand as a prop, and simply press *PAUSE* between each photo or when the urge strikes.

The macro setting on the lens lets you focus at extremely close distances to the subject, whether it's a photograph, a document, or an object. Securing the camera on a steady base and placing it between a pair of high-wattage household lightbulbs will provide an easy yet adequate setup.

Another method of mixing the old (film) with the new (video) is to put the camera to use in a different way. If you have home movies of your family, these can be transferred (as can color slides) to videotape with the camera and a telecine converter. The transfers could also be done professionally. Chances are there's a photogra-

It is best to mount the camera horizontally when copying photographs or other printed material. If the camera is mounted so it faces down, debris may fall toward the front of the Vidicon tube, causing black specks to show in the picture and possibly damage the tube.

phy or video outlet near your home that provides these services. If you don't know of one, consult your Yellow Pages under TV, film, photography, and/or other related listings.

You might want to open with a "talking head" shot of yourself taped by the camera as it is mounted on a tripod. Arrange your position so you face the TV and turn down the set's sound (to avoid ear-splitting feedback). Now you can watch your every move and correct unattractive posture problems or hand movements as you perform. This is using the TV screen as a video monitor.

While you're "on camera" it's a simple matter to hold the VCR's remote pause control out of sight. If you're alone, you can still stop the tape yourself without ever moving off camera and disrupting the continuity.

Have a little fun and put on a musical selection that gives your program a humorous tone. You can try honky-tonk music, or maybe majestic cuts from a movie's soundtrack album. For a really grand entrance, put on a "live" album and record only the audience's applause. While the hands are clapping feverishly, stroll into the framed scene and take a few bows. As the warm reception subsides, remotely pause the VCR, change the music to an instrumental, and resume your place on screen while releasing the remote pause button. You've just edited yourself back into the next scene.

There are any number of ideas and events that can be turned into engrossing subjects for your family album on videocassette.

You might want to record the events of your child's life. Start by recording the baby's birth. At measured intervals, the child's progress can be added to the tape, savoring such milestones of childhood as beginning to crawl, the first attempts to walk, and total triumph—baby's first words.

Take the portable to your child's Little League baseball or football game. You can record each at-bat or pass thrown. If the baseball isn't hit or the football caught, rewind the tape a little and get ready for the next time around.

In organized sports, video has become a popular training tool. After practice the coach plays back taped highlights of the team's play and of individual players. This form of instant feedback shows young athletes what their strong points are, which helps bolster confidence, and what part of their game needs refinement, which can instill discipline and humility.

Family participation in community events, birthday parties, a day at the fair, weddings, and so on can all be captured using the VCR as an electronic memory bank. You might shoot your guests as they walk in the door. (Warning, be selective as some people don't enjoy this sort of surprise with a camera, because it catches spontaneous reactions.) It often makes for entertaining video verité, however.

There are individuals who have visited relatives in a foreign country—it may be their ancestors' homeland—taking family album tapes along with them. You can regale family members in another land with shots of your home, your family cavorting outside, at a picnic, or delivering a special message directly to the relatives you're visiting.

When in a different country, you'll either have to take along your VCR and use a standard American TV set or have the cassette converted into the format standard of the country in which your family members live so you can leave them with the cassette. (Note, however, that such conversions can be expensive.)

INFORMATION STORAGE
Anyone who has ever been the victim of a burglary knows how difficult it can be to remember each and every item of value in their possession. As long as valuables are safe and sound, there's little to think about, but once they're gone, it becomes suddenly difficult, without a written record, to recall everything that might be missing. Video can help.

Insurance companies want descriptions of the stolen goods and may advise clients to keep a photographic record. A videotape of your valuables cannot stand as proof of ownership in and of itself, but it certainly will help you instantly remember and describe anything in your home, including your video equipment. Any expensive, easily moved item that can be quickly resold is a magnet for petty thieves, who are always looking for fast and easy cash in exchange for their newfound loot.

Take the camera and VCR (if portable) around your home, recording all the contents of your rooms and the immediate area outside as well.

A recommended procedure for beginning the visual insurance inventory is focusing on the day's date as printed in a newspaper. For smaller items and for capturing serial numbers on TVs and the like, employ the macro focus as explained earlier. This closeup setting is ideal for jewlery and other small valuables. As the camera "eyes" the item, you can describe it for the voice-over narrative. On playback, you can use the VCR's freeze frame to study closely a particular feature or possession.

Again, as suggested for the family album recording, you can use the camera's remote pause to turn off the VCR between shots, or you can let it record without interruption.

Photos and documents should be mounted or securely placed on a flat surface, with two light bulbs placed at 45-degree angles to provide sufficent light. When shooting this closely it may become necessary to move the camera, the object, or both until the picture is in sharp focus. Use as much light as possible to enhance the look of your subject. If you're short on available light sources, a properly placed piece of highly reflective material (such as Mylar) can heighten illumination without the need for additional lighting units.

Of course, once your insurance tape is complete make sure you keep it in a safe, secure spot where it won't be stolen.

HOME SECURITY

There are relatively simple ways using video equipment to ward off burglars and other potential intruders. Such defensive measures should keep your visual insurance record locked away so you will never have to use it as part of a statement for your insurance company.

Special closed-circuit TV (CCTV) cameras are low-light black-and-white units that can operate effectively in almost total darkness and are rugged enough to endure the natural elements.

A camera placed in the baby's nursery or other indoor location (such as in the kitchen, so you can watch a roast while you watch TV in the den) can be a standard model, since you don't have to keep it on for a long period of time.

The special advantages of CCTV cameras, though, are the remote control features available on certain models that allow you to activate the camera's zoom lens and horizontal or vertical movement from afar.

A camera can be mounted in a corner of the ceiling, on the wall, or on a tripod. You need extension cables for the camera. For the enterprising readers among you, the camera does not need to be routed through the VCR and then into the TV for monitoring. An RF converter allows you to connect the camera directly to the antenna terminals of the TV, freeing your VCR for off-air recording and playback duties.

OTHER APPLICATIONS

A video travelogue of your vacation is a good way to capture the atmosphere of a place—both its geography and its spirit. Just be sure to have on hand a sufficient supply of charged batteries for the portable, or bring along the separate AC-operated recharger. If you want to view the tapes right away, either use a camera with an electronic viewfinder that has playback capabilities or make sure you have the right connecting cables and any necessary adapters to hook up your VCR to the TV in your hotel or guest house.

If you're going to an exotic locale, be forewarned that certain cultures of the world recoil at the sight of a camera, especially if it's accompanied by a separate recorder. The more equipment, the quicker and more negatively the inhabitants may react.

Others have found video to be an effective medium at work as well as at play. In fact, some people have discovered its potential to help them land a job. In a performance-oriented profession like teaching, law, or any of the performing arts, including theatre, film, and TV work, and broadcast journalism, offering a sample of yourself in action will at least separate you from the other applicants for the position.

Many interviewers welcome a video resume, since it lets them screen prospects from distant cities while saving transportation costs. If you alert a personnel manager that you'll be sending along a videocassette of yourself, he or she may be able to offer specific qualities and qualifications that you can stress in your visual presentation.

Video is a highly versatile medium that extends substantially beyond the scope of simple entertainment. Once you've grown accustomed to the equipment and are comfortable with a camera in your hand, you'll soon find an endless number of ways in which video can enhance many aspects of your life.

7

VIDEO RECORDING — FROM THE PAST INTO THE FUTURE

THE PAST

Videotape recording was officially born in 1956, when Ampex Corporation demonstrated a video recording system that used two-inch (5 cm) wide tape, weighed almost two thousand pounds, and cost over fifty thousand dollars. Because it used four rotating tape heads to record and play back information, it was called Quadruplex, or simply Quad. It became the dominant medium for recording and playing back broadcast television signals.

Ten years later, Sony Corporation developed and introduced a half-inch black-and-white reel-to-reel portable video recorder, commonly known as a "portapak." Other makers followed suit, but none of the recorders were compatible. Tapes made on one brand could not be played back on another. The situation changed in 1969 when the Electronic Industries Association of Japan (EIAJ) induced manufacturers to standardize the machines. With standardization, the popularity of video recording skyrocketed. Schools, businesses, government agencies, advertising agencies, and independent artists took immediate advantage of the newly accessible recording medium. Standardization also resulted in improved picture quality and better overall engineering.

These popular portapaks used the now common "helical scan" method of videotape recording. The electronic tracks recorded on the tape and retrieved by the rotating heads of the tape player must be long enough to produce an acceptable picture. On the two-inch Quad machine, the tape was wide enough to allow tracks to be recorded perpendicular to the length of the tape. Tape narrower

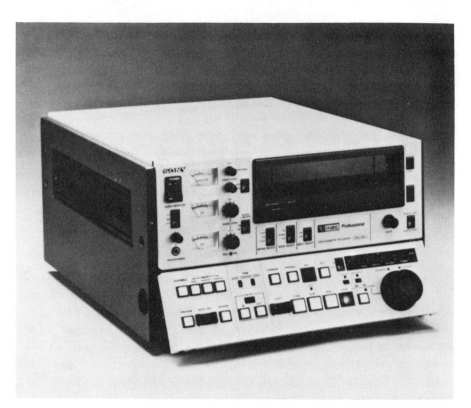

If you were taking a step beyond the ½-inch technology found in home video recording equipment, you'd find the popular U-Matic format, characterized by ¾-inch wide videotape. Pictured is a state-of-the-art 1982 model from Sony, who developed the U-Matic design. It's most commonly used by medical and educational institutions, insurance firms and other businesses with many branch offices across the country, advertising agencies, TV stations, and in other areas of communications.

than two inches could not accommodate tracks in the same fashion. The resulting design, to accommodate the half-inch tape—helical scan—has the recording tracks running on a diagonal from the bottom of the tape to the top.

In the early seventies, half-inch was further refined, with color, electronic editing, and lighter-weight portables added. Its low cost, simple operation, and production capabilities made the half-inch standard increasingly popular with non-broadcast users (it was not considered good enough for broadcasting).

Panasonic tried to make the format more convenient by putting the tape into a cartridge. It was compatible with the reel-to-reel models but importantly, it eliminated the user's having to thread tape. The cartridge was a moderate success, mostly with hospitals and some sales training networks, but it was preempted by yet another development from Sony. In 1969 the company introduced a new format to the industry using three-quarter-inch (1.9 cm) wide videotape. It was more sophisticated than half-inch, with superior electronic editing and production capabilities, and was contained in a convenient cassette. The wider tape also produced a better picture. A basic rule of thumb in video is that wider tape produces better pictures. The new format was soon standardized under the patented Sony trademark, U Matic. To this day, every three-quarter-inch videocassette recorder uses the U Matic design, and so all are compatible.

The acceptance of U Matic can be said to have taken place in 1972, when Ford Motor Company provided Sony a large order for U Matic equipment. Ford's stamp of approval is credited with giving videotape invaluable credibility as a communication medium for industrial users.

Originally, Sony thought U Matic to be an ideal home recording format, but at the request of its industrial users, the hardware became more and more sophisticated. It became evident that this format had become too advanced and too expensive to market to the home video user.

It's important to note that along the way, numerous oddball formats have been introduced, including incompatible half- and three-quarter- and even one-quarter-inch designs. None of these has survived as a standard because none offered anything special in the way of major features that could not be found in equipment already available in greater quantity.

The three-quarter-inch market is cornered today by Sony, Panasonic, and JVC. Cassettes come in lengths up to sixty minutes, with some extended-play ninety-minute tapes available.

Advertising agencies, hospitals, schools, businesses, government groups, organizations, and TV stations are all typical users of this equipment. It has had a major impact on TV station news departments, which favor its use over film for spot coverage. Three-quarter has even prompted the coining of a buzzword by TV people—"ENG," for Electronic News Gathering, or "EFP," for Electronic Field Production.

Originally touted as a convenient distribution system, three-quarter is also a versatile and effective production tool. Current models can be used with micro-processor-controlled random access units and offer still frame and stereo sound. Some models also have tuner timers to record off the air.

THE PRESENT

A new breed of half-inch equipment goes by the names Beta and VHS. Sony invented the Beta format, while Matsushita and JVC are patent holders of VHS, which stands for Video Home System. Matsushita, by the way, is the Japanese parent of Panasonic, Quasar and JVC.

Beta and VHS use slightly different mechanical approaches that render them incompatible. Sony introduced Betamax in late 1975, and VHS made its United States debut about one year later. Both systems use half-inch wide tape contained in a cassette. The VHS cassette is somewhat larger than the Beta, which is the most obvious difference and the reason for their lack of interchangeability. The two are so similar in function and features that it's easier and more accurate to consider them as the same format, or technology, using different designs. Both were built from the ground up as home recording machines.

Although no standardization formally exists for half-inch cassettes, many consider VHS the de facto standard simply because it commands 60 to 70 percent of the United States market.

Prices for Beta and VHS VCRs range from about five hundred to fifteen hundred dollars, depending upon features and where you shop. Blank cassettes cost fifteen to twenty-five dollars for a two-hour VHS tape, slightly less for the equivalent Beta. A good one-inch system costs about fifty-five thousand dollars and up. Two-inch (5.1 cm) Quad costs approximately one hundred thousand to one hundred-fifty thousand dollars, and is no longer better than one-inch systems.

For schools and small businesses, whose budgets are tight, half-inch offers cost benefits. Longer-playing tapes are available, and distribution of tapes is cheaper. The hardware is simpler to operate than three-quarter and less expensive to maintain. Most important, however, is that industrial versions of the two half-inch designs are being aggressively marketed by JVC and Panasonic for VHS, and by Sony for Beta.

These more rugged, better performing versions of the home half-inch decks are available as recorder/player or player-only models. They can interface with many of the same accessories used with U Matic systems. These include electronic editing consoles, digital random access keyboards, and other features for use in productions intended to be broadcast. The units also have two audio tracks for stereo or bilingual recording.

The advances in Beta and VHS industrial design have occurred in such a short span of time that they have to be considered serious threats to three-quarter-inch (1.9 cm) in the not too distant future. For production purposes, three-quarter will continue to be used. For distribution, though, programs are being dubbed onto the half-inch (1.3 cm) cassettes with increasing frequency.

Technology-based prospects for the eighties include the disappearance of at least two tape formats and the addition of at least one new format. The advent of digital video recording will enhance one-inch (2.5 cm) helical scan tape, which is already supplanting the outmoded two-inch Quad at the networks. Broadcasters are integrating one-inch systems into their production process. Standardized one-inch systems, sold by Sony, Ampex, RCA, NEC, and Hitachi, offer stereo sound tracks with Dolby, full broadcast editing capability, and still frame and slow motion. In fact, one-inch recorders are being used by the networks for stop-action and slow-motion replays on sports coverage. They are replacing the older, slow-motion magnetic disk equipment.

Recently introduced were broadcast quality Beta and VHS format self-contained videocamera/VCRs. These expensive, fifty-thousand dollar units are capable of producing instant, ready-to-air videotape.

Consumer versions of these machines have been announced formally by Sony Corporation and are under development by other manufacturers for release in the near future.

The concept of using electronics to replace film does not stop with video as we know it today. In the very near future, we will be able to buy video-based cameras that record "still" pictures on a small magnetic disk. This system, also under development by Sony and other manufacturers, will allow for up to 50 still photographs to be taken and recorded on a disk selling for about two and a half dollars. The camera will be adaptable to taking standard video pictures when connected to a VCR. In theory, it would be a still cam-

Although they are incompatible, Beta (bottom) and VHS (top) recorders often look very similar. Beta format models, however, are often slightly smaller than VHS machines, because the Beta cassette is physically smaller than the VHS cassette.

era, about the size and weight of a 35mm SLR also usable as a small scale, somewhat limited video camera.

The technology that allows these new developments lies in a device called a *CCD*—Charge Coupled Device. The CCD replaces the Vidicon tube used (with some variation in name and design) in all of today's videocameras. Because the CCD is both flat and small, the size of a postage stamp, it will significantly reduce the size and complexity of videocameras and will ultimately lower their cost.

The problem with current CCDs is that they can not resolve as much detail as traditional Vidicon tubes. Over time this shortcoming will be eliminated and the CCD will become as standard as the transistor became in replacing the vacuum tube.

Home video will continue to develop and do so at a faster pace than ever before because interest in video products is increasing daily. While it has taken only a few years to get from "ground zero" to where we stand today, it will take even less time to jump into what we are now calling the future.

In the meantime, we should not expect significant changes in the basic concepts of home video equipment or in their features. What we are seeing is a decrease in the size and weight of VCRs, and with CCDs, we will see the same in the land of video cameras.

We can expect video to become the photography of the future and to be an accepted part of everyone's life—not the hobby of a small group of interested and dedicated people.

THE FUTURE

H. G. Wells, master science fiction writer and futurist, once wrote of a "Time Machine" that could magically transport people and objects in a matter of seconds to a different time and place. Not even today's scientists, with all the tools of technological wizardry at their disposal, can design a real-life working model of such a wondrous vehicle, but there's no need to. By the end of this century, we may all have "time machines" in our homes, though some have suggested a more appropriate term would be "teleportation units."

The trick to teleportation lies not in physically transporting people and objects through space, but in using the most advanced forms of telecommunications—electronic video and audio devices— to send ideas, images, and information from one place to another.

The concept of teleportation is simply an elaborate extension of the futuristic home media center already taking shape in the United States, Japan, and other parts of the world.

Any preview of the future in home entertainment and information must be grounded in contemporary products and capabilities. At the time of this writing, the videocassette recorder remains the keystone to viewer control of TV programming, permitting the VCR owner to play back commercially prerecorded cassettes of feature films, special instructional and educational tapes, and other types of programs, as well as "bending" the previously fixed broadcast TV schedule by taping programs that may be viewed at any time. In addition, by attaching an electronic video camera to the recorder, a new, more efficient, superior form of home moviemaking becomes possible, supplanting the quickly fading 8mm film home movie system. Programs can also be played back over your TV through a videodisc player, offering picture and sound quality superior to any other current form of home video.

For its part, cable television offers viewers an array of different channels—up to fifty-two—while at the same time eliminating those picture problems (ghosts, signal interference) that plague through-the-air broadcasts.

Other increasingly common components in the home media center are personal computers, large-screen TVs, and electronic video games. All these elements will remain part of the media center but other emerging technologies will work together with them to dramatically transform the above electronic devices into a central information console that will provide each of us with the sustenance needed for daily existence.

Among the most critical space-age-inspired additions to the evolving telecommunications network are fiber optics, microprocessors, and satellites.

The first, as its name suggests, uses light waves sent through microscopic strands of glass fibers to transmit electronic signals. Fiber optics can be expected to replace existing telephone and cable TV lines, since it is a much more economical method of transmitting information and affords a higher quality of reception. A single laser light fiber can carry hundreds of different telephone conversations, requiring a fraction of the space, cost, and energy of electrical wires.

A microprocessor is the central processing unit of a minicomputer contained on a tiny chip of silicon, which can accept and act on a set of precoded instructions. These remarkable microbrains make it possible for you to program a VCR to automatically record different TV channels at different times when you're away from home, and for TV sets and other appliances to turn themselves on and perform other functions simply by reacting to your verbal command (voice recognition).

Satellites are already being used by pay-TV systems such as Home Box Office, and by networks for live news and sports events, to send video pictures great distances in a matter of seconds.

Homes without access to cable can be equipped with a satellite TV antenna on the roof to receive directly any number of programs that are sent via the high-flying electronic switchboard.

Without even delving too deeply into future forms of home video technology it becomes apparent that we'll be able to choose from an almost infinite variety of programs. There will be two primary methods of viewing the programming—through self-contained delivery systems such as videocassette recorders, videodisc players, and built-in personal computers and through external sources, including satellites, cable TV, and central computer bases.

In fact, the watchword of programming as we approach the end of this millennium is "narrowcasting"—programs designed to appeal to individual tastes, desires, and special interests. Our current view of television is defined as "broadcasting," which refers to information packaged for and delivered to a mass audience. If current trends in home viewing tell us anything about the future, it's that broadcasting will continue to give way to narrowcasting, just as general-interest magazines ultimately yielded to people's desire for special-interest publications.

Martin Polon, an audio and video consultant at UCLA, notes: "I see the future as a future of alternative inputs." What will those inputs offer us in the way of form and function? The possibilities are tantalizing.

With all these sources of information available to us in the comfort, privacy, and convenience of our homes, suitable video display screens will be required. Giant, wall-sized screens in the shape of flat panels will give us a panoramic view of the world with picture quality not yet possible in available big-screen setups. The picture will not be projected and no TV tubes will be used, accounting for the screen's thinness. Flat panel TV will also be commonplace in miniature versions, so a business executive can open an attache case, turn on the TV contained inside, and thanks to satellites, fiber optics, and other still undeveloped technologies, hold a video conference with associates in Europe, Asia, and Australia.

The video image on these improved screens will be sharper, more lifelike and will be reproduced in truer colors. These improvements are the result of adding more lines (totaling over 1000) to the picture, compared with the approximately 500 or 600 found in most TV systems today.

Along with a more lifelike picture will come two-channel stereo digital sound, with reproduction that current hi-fi systems don't begin to approach.

An optical-laser disc player will be used to play both video and audio discs. Though still being refined, the laser method of video-disc playback will be perfected in the coming years. Not only will the picture be frozen on a given frame, advanced a single frame at a time, be shown in fast or slow motion, and be scanned at many times the normal playback speed, but storage capacity of a single disc will increase markedly.

Thin foil videodiscs will be bound into print periodicals (as a form of advertising) ready to be removed and viewed, while maga-zines and other printed matter will actually be designed for distri-bution on disc. Department store catalogs, textbooks, and repro-duced works of art will all be in disc form.

Personal libraries will consist of books and videodiscs of favorite films, TV programs from the dim, distant "early days of broad-casting," popular-culture entertainment such as live theatre, and nonentertainment material such as self-improvement programs on cooking, dancing, tennis, and skiing.

Tied to the home's central computer, a videodisc on cooking will take you through the recipe's steps, automatically stopping along the way as you actually prepare the dish.

Meanwhile, in the playroom, fourteen-year-old Tommy will be constructing a working-model rocketship, following instructions from his personal computer terminal, and older sister Laura will be found posed in front of a large screen mounted on a portable con-veyor belt, practicing her ski turns as she follows on the screen a simulated environmental scene played back through a second videodisc unit.

In strategic locations around the house, auxiliary screens can display programs from any source, each working independently of the other. Screens with secondary pictures let you monitor the baby's nursery or the front door, where low-light-level cameras are placed to serve as security measures.

The computer will be set in the morning to record specified pro-grams and other material. Upon returning later in the day, a ran-dom access keyboard will be used to instantly "call up" any of the recorded material. At the press of a button, a hard-copy printer will deliver to your hands a text version of stock quotations, local food prices, the next day's weather report, and confirmation of air-line reservations for your upcoming vacation.

Prerecorded programs for the computer will store your holiday

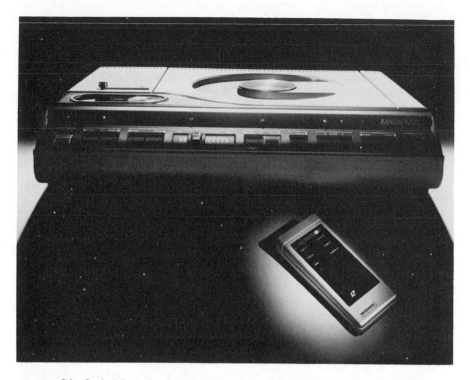

A new kind of video playback technology that we'll see more of in the future is the videodisc. The laserdisc, jointly developed by MCA and by N.V. Philips of The Netherlands (which owns Magnavox), offers the highest picture quality available from any home source, as well as stereo sound, and random access search of individual frames. The videodisc players currently available have one serious drawback, however, when compared with the videocassette machine: the videodisc can not record anything.

mailing list, letting you revise it at any time, and providing a printout of the list on labels or on regular paper. The electronic form of intelligence will also stand ready to challenge your intelligence with games that are preprogrammed or ones that you devise yourself. The possibilities are limitless.

If you want to prepare properly for your next marathon, tell the machine how many miles you have to run, how much you weigh, and other pertinent data: the computer will let you know, in short order, how much weight you should lose, what your exercise program should consist of, the type and quantity of food to eat during training, and how much the grocery bill will amount to.

Many of the functions of the electronic components described here will not have to be performed with levers, pushbuttons, or even "soft-touch" controls. Devices that respond to spoken commands (voice recognition or activation) and repeat the command to "say" something else such as "good morning, time to get up" (voice synthesis) will abound in the house. Tell the TV to "turn on, raise volume, select channel 6," and it will repeat back to you the order and proceed to do just that.

Supplementing the far-reaching capabilities of your home media center's built-in computer is the versatility of two-way cable television.

As the prototype for future systems, the Warner-Amex QUBE service holds the promise of providing us with almost every type of good and service imaginable.

Operating in Columbus (Ohio), Houston, Pittsburgh, and other cities, QUBE scans the house every six seconds to monitor for burglaries, fires, and other potentially dangerous occurrences. If it detects trouble, the proper local authorities (police, fire department, hospital) are notified of the house's location and the nature of the problem. In moments, help is on the way.

The QUBE central computer can also control a home's energy consumption by regulating major appliances to run at off-peak load hours (turning a dishwasher on at night automatically) and by regulating temperature flow. Warner-Amex Cable has estimated this kind of two-way computer housekeeping can save a property owner up to 30 percent in energy costs.

Two-way television also lets the viewer vote for local officials and register opinions on issues by pushing buttons on a multipurpose keypad. The writer Alvin Toffler has called this rare kind of citizen participation the best opportunity for "direct democracy" he has observed.

A variation on the theme of two-way, or interactive, television is *teletext*. Sent to your TV on an unused portion of the transmission signal, teletext is a central data base containing thousands upon thousands of pages of information, ranging from travel and entertainment directories to traffic, weather, and news reports.

Operating in tandem with the telephone, teletext will also manage your budget by writing checks and transferring funds from your account to your creditors. If certain teletext information requires you to pay for it, the charge can be attached to your telephone bill.

Going one step beyond, two-way television will be used to order goods you normally would go out to purchase. Using a keypad to "view" the catalog or sales information of a certain store, you can either order via a special computer code (which will have the bill sent to you) or insert a magnetic credit card in a slot and you'll automatically be charged for your purchase.

Cable systems equipped with 100 or more channels, a task made simpler and cheaper with fiber optics, will become more responsive to individual viewers with the offering of academic telecourses for credit, coverage of local government sessions, the showcasing of school sports that otherwise would not receive coverage and, as noted above, the provision of information and services now mostly confined to newspaper and other printed matter.

The Yellow Pages and classified advertising are two prominent examples of how video will provide consumer services more cost-effectively and efficiently.

Fiber optic inputs also will allow the home's central computer to gain access to other computers, to communicate with individuals by videophone (or "picturephone"), to send and receive printed messages that are also displayed on-screen (electronic mail), and to play video games long-distance with a friend or a complete stranger in a city far away. There are even more mind-boggling applications and functions of the future home media center.

Videocassette records built into tubeless video cameras are being developed faster than expected. Original live-action recordings will be made through these extremely lightweight, portable cameras. The micro-videocassette can then be played back over a portable video monitor at a remote location—all you need carry is that TV-equipped attache case—or on the wraparound screen in the central media area of your home.

For more-enterprising creative types, advanced, inexpensive production equipment is worth anticipating. Abstract or realistic images can be created and designed with laserform generators to achieve three-dimensional holograms that seem to appear out of thin air in the middle of your room. A telepalette will enable budding artists to turn the screen into an electronic canvas, drawing from the same primary and mixed colors available to an artist working with oil or watercolor paints.

Video synthesizers, mixers, editing consoles, and other production equipment will greatly enhance the style and content of original "videograms," to an extent amateur home filmmakers never would have dreamed possible.

If all this doesn't dazzle you, consider another outgrowth of high technology (going on in aerospace research labs) that someday will enter the home. As you are listening to a favorite musical piece on your digital audio system, you plug on a headset outfitted with electrode sensors and place it atop your head. As you visualize the music in your mind's eye, what you are imagining begins to assume visible form in front of your eyes. If your thoughts turn to a remote, serene South Seas island, that is precisely the environment you will seem to be in.

If you're thinking South Seas and end up crawling through the desert towards an illusory oasis, don't blame it on the technology, and don't complain to your travel agent. Just call in the teleportation unit repair man to replace your faulty electrodes.

It may sound a lot like H. G. Wells, but none of this is science fiction. What you've just read, believe it or not, will become scientific fact.

8

VIDEO GAMES, HOME COMPUTERS, AND VIDEODISC PLAYERS

Throughout this book the authors have discussed primarily the home VCR and video camera. This is, after all, the equipment that made home video possible and is the most complex of all gear to operate properly. But there are a number of other types of home video equipment.

HOME COMPUTERS AND VIDEO GAMES
Home computers and video games are two closely related and popular types of home video equipment. In fact, the more advanced home video games are actually computers, but preprogrammed ones with limited functions. Connecting a home computer or home video game to a television screen is simplicity itself. Accessory devices are commonly available in computer and electronics stores that allow you to make the proper connections from your specific home computer to your television set or video system. Video game consoles, not actual game cartridges, usually come supplied with small switch boxes that enable similar connections to your television set or video system.

VIDEODISC PLAYERS
Another popular piece of home video equipment is the videodisc player. Videodisc players simply plug into the antenna (VHF *IN-*

put) connector of your TV set or VCR. Some disc players feature connectors that allow you to input their video and audio signals directly into your TV set or monitor, bypassing the RF stages.

There are two types of videodisc systems currently available. The first, the Laservision (LV) system, developed jointly by Philips and MCA, uses a beam of low-powered laser light to read the information imbedded under the surface of the mirrorlike 12-inch videodisc. The primary benefit of the LV system is the incredibly high quality of the picture. In use, it has sharpness, clarity, and color saturation superior to just about any other signal source available to your television set. In addition, many LV discs are recorded in stereo, and when the player is connected to a hi-fi system, the sound quality is almost as good as that of a standard LP phonograph record.

Since their introduction, LV discs have come a long way. Originally plagued by quality-control problems, today's discs are remarkably improved and a genuine treat for the eye and ear. Playing time has been standardized at one-hour per side for movies, eliminating most of the highly touted special features of still frame, slow motion, reverse playing, variable play speeds, etc., but increasing playing convenience. Interactive discs, those which allow the viewer to participate in the program being viewed, are becoming more readily available, and these discs allow the LV system to utilize all the special effects it is known for. Like all disc playing systems, the primary disadvantage is that you cannot record with the system. But the picture and sound quality of the system when playing prerecorded material makes it certainly worth considering.

The second videodisc system is commonly called CED. This format, developed and marketed by RCA and its licensees, is an altogether different engineering approach. It is a needle-in-groove system. Reading capacitance changes recorded into the surface of the disc, the CED system traces its signals very much like an ordinary record player. The disc, because it is highly sensitive to dust and fingerprint grease or any other surface aberrations, is encased in a caddy and is never actually seen or touched by the user. The player removes the disc from the caddy, and the caddy must be inserted into the player to remove the disc from the player. It's a totally hands-off system. Neither the picture nor the sound quality of the CED disc system is as good as that of the LV system. Compared to prerecorded videotape, the CED system sometimes achieves parity with the better-quality tapes but is more consistent in its performance than is tape.

The most obvious advantage of either disc system over a tape system is that the software (the actual discs) costs a third to half as much as prerecorded tape. This is not an important consideration if you plan to only rent videotapes, but if you plan to buy them it is of major importance.

The Laservision system costs a good deal more than the CED system at retail, although list prices can be deceiving, and the cost of the LV discs is generally higher, but not by so much that it should enter into the purchase decision. The CED system (as of this writing) has a greater library of material upon which to draw, but this is a fluid situation. Manufacturers who back each system are constantly signing on new software suppliers. If you are considering a videodisc system, and the choice is between the two, CED gets the nod for the cost-conscious consumer, LV for the purist. It is not fair to directly compare the two systems because the only similarity is that they both play videodiscs. The LV system was designed for, and is marketed to, the connoisseur; the CED system is designed for the mainstream, cost-conscious consumer.

Attaching a videodisc player to a video system is simple. Both systems can be attached by connecting a cable from the videodisc's VHF *OUT*put to the VHF *IN*put of a TV set. The LV videodisc player, however, offers the additional feature of allowing you to connect the video output directly to the video *IN*put of a monitor or TV set and the audio output directly into a stereo system. Soon CED will have stereo capability but it will, most likely, never be able to match the LV system in terms of picture quality or special features.

A third system, VHD, may be on the market shortly after the first printing of this book. If it does make it to the market, it will resemble a hybrid of the LV and CED systems' technologies. It will have virtually all the same features as LV systems and it will be priced more in line with CED. It will be a capacitance system, using a form of needle, as CED does. However, the VHD system needle will not actually make physical contact with the surface of the disc. The needle will ride just above the surface, and therefore, as in LV systems, disc wear will not be a factor in normal use.

Two educational videodiscs are shown. In the foreground a popular
Laservision selection, in the background a typical CED choice. In the
background are two Laservision players on the left and a CED player on
the right. Flanking the large screen television are two loudspeaker systems that enable the videodisc systems to reproduce "movie-like quality"
entertainment in the home.

A FINAL THOUGHT

Whether or not your video system will utilize a video game, computer, or videodisc player now or at sometime in the future depends upon how much of this technology you wish to be able to enjoy and, of course, how much of it you can afford to purchase.

Video is not a cheap source of home entertainment, although some very real bargains can be found through careful shopping. It is, however, an investment from which you can reap untold benefits as it broadens your world of "home" entertainment and knowledge. Previously we discussed the history of video from the past into the future. For the most part, much of the future is here now, and you can enjoy much of what is envisioned in some form today. Large-screen television sets (projection TVs) have come of age, have been perfected. You can, have, at a cost, a ten-foot picture in your living or "media" room today.

Video products will, as all electronic products, continue to improve or, in some cases, become less expensive to purchase. Home computers should become more common, and soon video games will be found in almost every home.

The basics of home video explained in this volume will hold well into the future. Technological advances will not alter the basics, only mitigate or improve upon them. It is, for example, doubtful that an instruction manual written for a 1950s color TV would be so out-of-date that it could not be used today. The instructions basically still apply, even with the technological advances that have been made over the past thirty years. If in the near future a CCD replaces a Vidicon tube, the video camera will still work the same way; it will only be smaller and lighter or perhaps somewhat less expensive to buy.

Having read and understood this book, you are well prepared for the future and certainly well armed for any video happenstance you may have to face today or tomorrow.

RECORD/PLAYBACK TIMES AVAILABLE IN BETA & VHS BY TAPE LENGTH AND SPEED (TIME IN MINUTES)

BETA FORMAT*

SPEED	L-125	L-250	L-370	L-500	L-750	L-830
Beta I	15	30	45	60	90	***
Beta II	30	60	90	120	180	200
Beta III	45	90	135	180	270	300

   * With most Beta Tape brands, the numerical designation in the label refers to meters of tape contained within the cassette. An L-500 contains 500 meters of tape.

*** Not recommended for use at this speed.

VHS FORMAT**

SPEED	T-30	T-60	T-90	T-120	T-180****
SP	30	60	90	120	180
LP	60	120	180	240	360
SLP	90	180	270	360	540

  ** Most brands of VHS cassettes are labeled to indicate playing time in minutes at the standard SP playing speed. A T-120 provides 120 minutes (or two-hours) of record/playback time at the SP speed.

****Not available to consumers as of this writing. May not be recommended at all VHS tape speeds.

GLOSSARY OF VIDEO TERMS

Air—The medium of transmission of radio waves. To record "off the air" is to record material being transmitted.

Audio dub—Replacing an existing sound track with another.

Aperture—The width of a lens relative to its focal length. The adjustable control for the amount of light passing through a lens or light fixture. Usually the size of the aperture is expressed as an *f*-stop—*f*/1.6, *f*/22, etc. Also called iris.

Beta—The ½-inch videocassette format developed by SONY.

Bootleg—A program—most typically a videocassette—that is duplicated, distributed, and sold by unauthorized agents. Also known as piracy, punishable as a federal offense. Characteristically, bootleg tapes of popular feature films are noticeably below the quality of those tapes commercially licensed for home video purchase or rental by the copyright holders.

Break-up—Picture distortion that results in an indecipherable image, lasting a few seconds.

Cable TV—Any system whereby televised images are sent by co-axial cable (wire). There is usually a fee for this service.

Cassette—A two-reel container for tape or film.

CED—Capacitance Electronic Disc. RCA's patented videodisc system that employs a diamond stylus to read video and audio information encoded in the disc's grooves as it spins at 450 rpm.

Channel—A broadcast or cable frequency, assigned to TV or cable stations by the Federal Communications Commission.

Color bars—The industry standard reference designed by the Society of Motion Picture and Television Engineers (SMPTE) for the levels and phasings of original recordings. Test bars are electronically generated and accompanied by a 1,000 Hz audio reference tone.

Convergence—The method by which three primary colors for television (red, blue, and green) are made to overlap perfectly to form an ideal color image.

Converter box—Special TV tuner supplied by cable companies that enables cable channels to be tuned by home TVs.

Copy guard—A signal on recorded video material that prevents unauthorized duplications by effectively weakening the sync signal. The technique was developed by producers of legitmate copyrighted programming to prevent piracy.

Crispness—The sharpness (focus) of the televised picture.

CRT—Cathode Ray Tube. The standard TV picture tube.

Descrambler—A device that unscrambles specially encoded pay TV signals.

Display—A device that shows computer output or status visually but not on paper, usually a CRT or a multi-segment LED system similar to that of a calculator.

Dissolve—To fade into a scene while fading out the on-screen image.

Distortion—Electronic interference in video.

Dropout—A momentary absence of a video or an audio signal usually caused by a tape or disc surface irregularity.

Dub—To duplicate audio or video. Recordings made by connecting one recorder to another. A dub is one generation removed from the copy it is made from. (Also called dupes.)

Edit—To manipulate program material to a desired end by eliminating and/or rearranging it.

Electron gun—A device that emits a continous beam of electrons that is focused on the TV screen within the cathode ray tube.

Erase—To electronically remove information from tape.

EVF—Electronic viewfinder. Small TV monitor attached to a video camera allowing a scene to be viewed exactly as it will appear on tape.

Fade—To bring the video picture on or off the screen slowly.

Focus—To adjust the lens to film distance based on the lens to subject distance, to produce a sharp image on the film.

Format—The width of videotape:
- 2-inch reel-to-reel or quad; used only by TV studios.
- 1-inch professional applications, used increasingly by TV stations.
- ¾-inch U-Matic (cassette system): Considered superior to ½ inch tape and used primarily by business, educational institutions, and advertising agencies.
- ½-inch: There are two incompatible ½-inch systems—the Beta system (developed by SONY) and the VHS system (developed by JVC).

Generally speaking, the wider the tape, the better the picture quality.

Freeze frame—A feature of videocassette recorders and disc players. It allows the user to stop the tape or disc and maintain a static image on the monitor. This is an option on videocassette recorders and is standard on the optical-laser videodisc system. It is not available with the capacitance videodisc system.

F-Stop—Industry notation for lens aperture size. The smaller the *f*-number, the larger the opening—i.e. *f*/1.6 is larger than *f*/8.

Gain—The luminance or whiteness level of a video image.

Generation—The master is the original: a dub from the master is first generation, etc.

Graphics—Titles and the like, also means the processing and output of pictures, diagrams, and visual abstractions by a computer.

Hardware—The video equipment itself as opposed to its programs (software).

Head—An electromagnetic device used to convert signals on tape to audio or video images or vice versa.

Hertz (Hz)—Cycles per second.

Hiss—Continuous noise from the high end of the frequency band that can be heard during tape playback.

Hue—The overall color emphasis of the video image. If the picture is bluish, greenish, or reddish, the hue or tint is not adjusted properly (professionally known as color phase).

Hum—Low-frequency noise.

Impedance—A measure of the resistance of electron flow in an electronic circuit.

Interactive—Refers to type of video program that lets the viewer participate in the program in a manner other than from start to finish. This is possible because of special computer encoded features in the video program.

Interlace—A television set's ability to display accurately spaced horizontal lines.

Line Scan—The sweep of the electron beam across the picture tube. In the United States, the broadcast standard calls for 525 sweeps to each frame.

Luminance—The intensity of brightness of a picture tube.

LV—LaserVision. The Philips-MCA patented videodisc system that employs laser-optics to read video and audio information encoded in the disc's microscopic pits as it spins.

Monitor—For video/television: receiver used in closed-circuit systems or professional TV studios, where the video signal is electronically connected to the CRT screen. The only difference between a monitor and a conventional television set is that use of the monitor does not entail the use of an RF adaptor (see RF adaptor).

Noise—Any kind of electronic interference.

NTSC—National Television Standards Commission. Broadcast standard in North America and other places. It calls for 525 line scans per frame.

Overscan—The difference in size between the TV picture tube and the picture it displays. TV manufacturers deliberately make pictures bigger because as picture tubes age, the size of their picture shrinks. Most sets overscan by about 15% when new.

PAL—Phase Alternating Line System. The broadcast standard in Europe and other places. It calls for 625 line scans per frame, which gives the PAL picture more detail and resolution than the NTSC 525 line scans per frame standard.

Piracy—Illegal duplication and sale of prerecorded programs (See Bootleg).

Prerecorded program—A program (eg. movie, TV show, concert, stage play, instructional film) commercially duplicated and distributed on a self-contained format such as videocassette or videodisc.

Primary colors—The three colors used to make up the color television picture: red, blue, and green.

Program—(See "Software").

Programmable VCR—A videocassette recorder than can be preset to record more than one program, on separate channels, for a future recording.

Projection TV—There are two types of projection TV. The one-lens system places a lens in front of a conventional TV set (usually 12- or 13-inch), which then focuses the enlarged picture onto a reflective screen.

The other projection TV system employs three projection tubes (red, blue, and green), which concentrate light-beam energy onto a reflecting screen, producing a more vivid (brighter, higher resolution) image than the single-lens system.

Public domain—Noncopyrighted material. Anyone has the right to reproduce in print or electronically.

Random access feature—A feature of videodisc players and videocassette recorders which allows the user to quickly pinpoint the location of a piece of programming material on tape or disc. This is considered a high-priced option and is not standard, but is available on videocassette recorders. Random access is standard on the optical videodisc system and is not available on the capacitance system.

Rear projection—A form of large-screen television where the image is projected from behind onto a screen that is otherwise viewed normally.

RF Adaptor (radio frequency)—A device that converts the incoming broadcast signal into a form that can be received by the television receiver.

Search feature—A feature of the videocassette recorder and optical videodisc system that speeds through programming material while it appears at high speed on the monitor. This is optional on VCR's and standard on the optical disc system.

SECAM—Sequential Couleur A Menoir. The broadcast standard in France and the Soviet Bloc. It's similar to the PAL standard in that it requires 625-lines per frame.

Signal-to-noise ratio—The ratio between picture and sound information and the inherent noise in the equipment reproducing it. The higher the ratio between the signal (which carries the picture) and the noise (distortion or snow), the better the picture.

Snow—One type of television interference—it looks like a blizzard on the picture.

Software or program—The vehicle, in our case usually a videocassette, that can carry information, or already has information on it, for playback.

Switcher/fader—A control device that permits the hookup of more than one camera into the video system. The fader permits the gradual transition from one camera to another (called crossfade).

Tape generation—Duplications made from a master or original (audio and video). A copy made from the master is called the first generation, and so forth. Usually, the quality of each succeeding generation is poorer.

Terminal—A device with a keyboard and a display screen (CRT) or printer, through which a computer and a human being can communicate.

Time shift—The ability to watch a program at a time other than when it was broadcast.

Transmission—The broadcast of electronic signals.

Tuner—A device that adjusts the frequency (channel) received by a TV or radio. All TV's have two tuners: VHF and UHF.

UHF—The Ultra-High Frequency broadcast band containing channels 14 through 83 on most TV's.

VCR—Videocassette Recorder. A type of video tape recorder (see VTR) that uses ¾, ½, or ¼-inch videocassettes to record and play back video information via a television receiver or monitor.

VHD—Video High Density. JVC/Matsushita's patented videodisc system that employs a sapphire stylus to read video and audio information encoded in a grooveless disc as it spins at 900 RPM.

VHD/AHD—Video high density/audio high density. Videodisc technology that provides special playback effects such as slow motion, fast motion and freeze frame as well as stereo sound. This technology uses a stylus pick-up system. Used in Quasar and JVC's videodisc systems to be introduced in 1982.

VHF—The Very High Frequency broadcast band containing channels 2 through 13 on most TV's.

VHS—The ½-inch videocassette format developed by JVC. VHS stands for Video Home System.

Videodisc—There are currently two incompatible disc formats— the optical-laser read system and the capacitance system. Both systems use discs that resemble long-playing records. However, in the laser-read system the information is sandwiched between two clear layers of plastic. The optical stylus never comes in contact with the disc. Therefore, theoretically, the disc will never wear out. The capacitance disc has its information on the surface, which comes in contact with the pickup system and is susceptible to the same hazards as conventional audio records.

Videodisc player—A unit resembling an audio phonograph, used to play back both audio and video signals. The LV optical-laser system employs a low-power laser beam directed by a series of lenses to bounce off the surface of the disc and reflect onto a optical pickup system. This then interprets the reflected audio and video signals. The pickup system does not come in contact with the surface of the disc.

The RCA CED (capacitance electronic disc) system employs a stylus that tracks the surface of the disc, as in an audio phonograph system. The audio and video signals are picked up in this manner.

A third videodisc design has been developed by JVC (Victor Company of Japan) and adapted by its parent company, Matsushita. The JVC system, called VHD (Video High Density), combines some of the advantages of both of the above technologies. It reads the videodisc with a stylus, as in RCA's capacitance system and has such features as freeze frame, search, and slow motion.

Video monitor—A CRT display screen, usually similar to a TV screen but without a tuner, used for the direct connection of a video signal without an RF adaptor.

Video modulator—A device to convert straight video signals (that could be fed to a video monitor or video recorder) into modulated signals that a regular TV set can receive (an RF circuit).

VTR—Videotape recorder—usually employing open-reel, one or two-inch, broadcast-quality videotapes as compared to videocassettes, which are used primarily in the home.

INDEX